SPOTLIGHT

EUGENE, SALEM
& THE WILLAMETTE VALLEY

JUDY JEWELL & W. C. McRAE

Contents

EUGENE, SALEM
& THE WILLAMETTE VALLEY

EUGENE, SALEM & THE WILLAMETTE VALLEY

The Willamette Valley, which was the main destination of the Oregon Trail pioneers, is one of the most productive agricultural areas in the world. This is something that is meaningful not only to long-ago pioneers or present-day residents, but to nearly every visitor. Wineries abound, as do plant nurseries and U-pick berry fields. During the spring, the tulip and iris fields are beautiful, especially when (as is not uncommon) they're backed up by a rainbow. Superb green beans, the highest-yielding sweet corn in the United States, and grass seed and hazelnuts that dominate world markets compound the impression of pastures of plenty.

The Willamette Valley is also the population center of Oregon, supporting 100 cities and 70 percent of the state's population. (Geographically speaking, Portland is part of the Willamette Valley, but it has its own chapter in this book.) Nonetheless, once you get south of Portland's suburbs, you'll seldom have the feeling of being in a big metropolis, which is partly thanks to the state's land-use regulations, which have historically sought to preserve agricultural land.

This mix of environmental conservation, excellent growing conditions, and culture is probably best exemplified by the phenomenal success of the winemaking industry. Best known for the cool-climate wine grapes, Oregon's handcrafted wines are produced in small lots rather than corporate quantities.

PLANNING YOUR TIME

Although it's only about 100 miles from Portland to Eugene, it's worth taking some

© JUDY JEWELL

HIGHLIGHTS

◀ **Carlton:** Although wine grapes are now grown all over the state, the area around Carlton in Yamhill County is a great place to tour some of the nation's top pinot noir and pinot gris wineries. Look at a map and choose your route to avoid busy Highway 99W (page 16).

◀ **State Capitol:** If a visit to the capitol seems like something that you should've gotten out of the way in grade school, think again. The art alone in the Oregon capitol building is worth the trip (page 24).

◀ **Mount Angel Abbey:** The hilltop abbey is a good place for both quiet reflection and architectural tourism; the splendid abbey library was designed by famed Finnish architect Alvar Aalto (page 35).

◀ **Silver Falls State Park:** Aren't waterfalls what Oregon is all about? Here a seven-mile trail passes 10 waterfalls (page 37).

◀ **Breitenbush Hot Springs:** The rest of the world will slip away as you ease yourself into one of the lovely natural hot pools. Come for an organized yoga or spiritual retreat, a weekend of personal reflection, or simply an afternoon soak. Clothing, however, is a seldom-used option in the hot springs (page 38).

◀ **Alton Baker Park:** This sprawling park, just across the Willamette River from downtown and the university, is home to Pre's Trail, a four-mile trail commemorating the late great runner Steve Prefontaine. The park's trail network hooks up with other running, walking, and biking trails – these trails along the Willamette and up into the nearby hills are a large part of what makes Eugene such a pleasant livable place (page 56).

◀ **McKenzie River National Recreation Trail:** Ride the city bus (or drive your car) up the McKenzie River to the start of this 26-mile trail. The McKenzie is a magical river, with waterfalls cascading over lava rocks and lush green streamside vegetation (page 74).

◀ **Oakridge Mountain Biking:** In the hills just outside this working-class mill town, you'll find some of the state's best mountain biking (page 80).

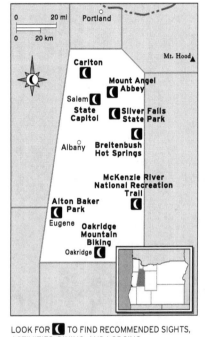

LOOK FOR ◀ TO FIND RECOMMENDED SIGHTS, ACTIVITIES, DINING, AND LODGING.

time to explore the back roads and smaller towns off I-5. For starters, plan to spend at least one day and a night in the north Willamette Valley's **wine country.** By spending the night you'll get to really relax and enjoy a dinner at one of several excellent restaurants in the area. For most travelers, McMinnville makes a good overnight stop; if you want a luxurious resort, Newberg's Allison Inn is your spot.

It's also worth spending a night or two in Eugene, both to experience the town and to explore the river valleys and west slopes of the Cascades that lie to the east of town.

Campers who are also oenophiles can pitch a tent at Champoeg State Park; it's in an area rich with pioneer history as well as being reasonably close to wineries. If hiking is more your focus, head to Silver Falls State Park, home to 10 large waterfalls and within striking distance of the Oregon Garden and lovely Mount Angel Abbey.

THE LAND

Within 50 miles of the fertile Willamette Valley are the Pacific Ocean to the west and the Cascade Mountain Range to the east. At the north, or downstream, end of the Willamette is Portland, and to the south (beyond Eugene) are the Rogue and Umpqua Valleys. East of Eugene, up the McKenzie River and the Middle Fork of the Willamette, the land rises toward the western slopes of the Cascades.

The Native Americans who first lived in the area never cultivated the soil or logged, save for burning to provide browse for deer and soils for grasses, roots, and berries. But centuries of fire in the valley had cleared the land of trees and set the stage for the current agricultural colossus. This practice exposed rich alluvial soils deposited by floods thousands of years ago—earth that is ideal for farming.

The first Europeans who came here in the second decade of the 1800s declined to take advantage of the prime farmland, preferring instead to reap easy money from the fur trade. It fell to the Oregon Trail influx in the mid-19th century to break ground for the present-day agricultural success story.

HISTORY

Before the white settlers arrived, the Kalapuya people lived in this fertile area for centuries, supplied with endless amounts of game, berries, camas (a lily-like perennial with a sweet bulbous root), wapato tubers, and fish. All the evidence suggests that the Willamette Valley people had achieved a remarkably stable equilibrium with their environment. The ancestors of these people were most likely the first settlers in the valley.

They moved seasonally, wintering in the area for more than 5,000 years. Although an estimated 80,000 Kalapuyas once dwelled here, their numbers decreased in the early 19th century due to exposure to diseases brought in by non–Native American explorers and traders.

The first European Americans arrived in 1812, and numbers swelled in the middle part of the century as Oregon Trail pioneers settled the area. To early white settlers, this place offered a second chance and a stage upon which to play out their most cherished economic, civic, educational, and cultural impulses.

The progressive orientation of the 1960s and 1970s arose from the Willamette River area's history. Once the river became the transport route for valley produce to Portland en route to gold rush–era San Francisco, prosperity and people coalesced around its shores. A century later, 20 municipalities and more than 600 industrial plants along the river had so befouled the waters that Governor Tom McCall described it as an "open sewer." The next decade's Willamette Greenway legislation put $50 million and the efforts of industry toward a cleanup. The results were the first significant salmon spawning runs in 40 years and a spate of riverfront parks and recreation areas. Although this environmental legacy has not escaped untrammeled, it is still an almost entirely pleasant experience to tour the Willamette via canoe.

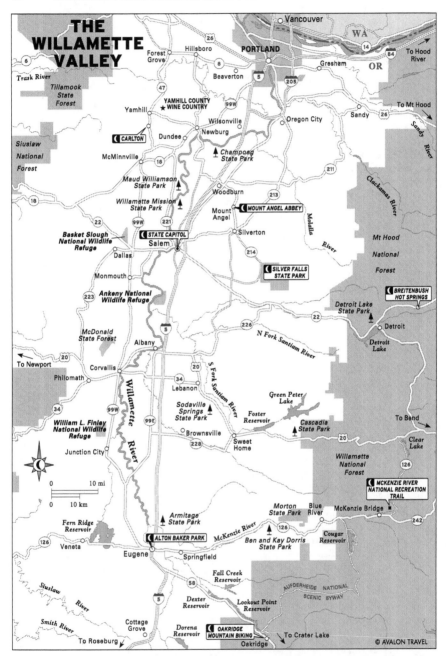

© AVALON TRAVEL

Wine Country

Although there's an increasing amount of excellent wine made in southern Oregon and in the Columbia Gorge, Oregon's wine country is generally thought to include those vineyards west and southwest of Portland in Yamhill County. This is where the rich soil and long gentle growing season have created conditions that sustain the largest concentration of vineyards in the Northwest. The slow-cooling fall days engender a complexity in the regional product by inhibiting high sugar concentrations while maintaining the natural acidity of the grape. In summer, Oregon's northern latitude makes for long sunny days without excessive heat, a condition that bodes well for the harvest. These factors combine to produce wines delicate in flavor, low in alcohol, and crisp in finish, despite a tendency toward fruitiness.

A good website that focuses on Willamette Valley wines is www.willamettewines.com. Tasting rooms in Oregon range from no-frills makeshift back rooms to relatively grand affairs. Some of the best wineries don't even maintain regular tasting rooms, but just about every place opens its doors during Thanksgiving and Memorial Day weekends, the two best (though most crowded) times to sample a really wide range of excellent wines.

The only better opportunity to taste pinot noirs, made from the region's signature grape, is at the annual **International Pinot Noir Celebration** (503/472-8964 or 800/775-4762, www.ipnc.org). More than 60 American and international pinot noir producers are on hand for symposia, tastings, and winery tours. Meals prepared by internationally known chefs are also a highlight. The three-day event takes place at the end of July on the Linfield College campus in McMinnville. While the cost of registration, $975, is prohibitive for all but the most serious oenophiles, tickets to the final tasting can be purchased separately for $125. Register well in advance; this event always sells out.

Tasting and Touring

Willamette Valley wineries and tasting rooms are generally open 11 A.M.–5 P.M. daily, but if you have your heart set on visiting a particular winery, it's always a good idea to call in advance to confirm hours and other details. Blue-and-white signs on Route 99W and its offshoots help point the way to such pantheons of pinot as Erath, Sokol Blosser, Yamhill Valley, and Amity.

Good wine and good food go together, which explains the creation of some surprisingly sophisticated restaurants in this very rural area. Wine touring is also popular because downtown Portland sits a mere 30–40 miles away from the state's greatest concentration of wineries. Just take I-5 south of the city and go west on Route 99W, and within 45 minutes you'll find yourself in the midst of filbert orchards and grapevines. In terms of distance, this might evoke wine-touring routes from San Francisco to the Napa and Sonoma Valleys, but the similarity ends there. Don't expect extensive tours of Oregon wineries and on-site restaurants. Nevertheless, as the Oregon wine country grows in popularity, weekend traffic gets worse every year. Hiring a car and driver or a tour company is becoming an increasingly appealing (and safer) alternative for many wine enthusiasts.

YAMHILL COUNTY WINE COUNTRY

Yamhill County and, to a somewhat lesser extent, adjoining Washington County are thick with wineries. Although this is known as one of the major pinot noir–producing regions in the world, the area's local wineries also produce pinot gris, pinot blanc, chardonnay, Riesling, Gewürztraminer, sparkling wine, sauvignon blanc, cabernet, and merlot.

You'll note that this tour starts west of Portland in Forest Grove and heads south from there. As much as we love exploring the wine country, we hate driving Route 99W. This tour

Many Willamette Valley wineries have picnic areas; an exceptionally lovely one is at Willakenzie Estate.

largely avoids it. To return to Portland without driving in 99W traffic, get a good road map and from Amity make your way east to the little town of Hopewell and the Wheatland Ferry. Ride the tiny car ferry across the Willamette (and notice here that you're in hop-growing territory) and continue east, following signs to I-5.

Forest Grove

The northernmost reach of the Willamette Valley's wine country is in Forest Grove, about 20 minutes west of Portland. Here you'll find **Shafer Vineyard Cellars** (6200 NW Gales Creek Rd., 503/357-6604) on a pretty oak-shaded hillside. In addition to pinot noir, Shafer makes sparkling wines and a few Rieslings, including an ice wine.

Don't leave Forest Grove without stopping in at **Sake One** (820 Elm St., 503/357-7056) to taste the local sake and tour the sakery. The sakes, made from California rice, range from the delicate Noma sake, a fresh unpasteurized wine that's available only at the tasting room,

to the milky coconut-scented Pearl or a clean-tasting, very slightly fruity Asian pear sake.

Montinore Estate (3663 Dilley Rd., 503/359-5012) is just south and west of downtown Forest Grove. As is the practice at many Willamette Valley vineyards, the grapes are grown sustainably using biodynamic practices.

Gaston

South of Forest Grove on Route 47, Gaston is home to **Elk Cove Vineyard** (27751 NW Olson Rd., 503/985-7760), one of the oldest and most respected operations in the area. Elk Cove's tasting room is especially lovely, and year-in and year-out their pinot gris is one of the region's best.

Yamhill

At Yamhill, head east of Route 47 on Route 240 to find, in a beautiful rural setting, the hillside vineyards of **Willakenzie Estate** (19143 NE Laughlin Rd., 503/662-3280). The three-level gravity-fed design of the winery (a tradition in Burgundy) allows gentle handling of the wine. Along with several different estate-grown pinot noirs, the tasting room pours a lush pinot gris and a crisp pinot blanc. Don't miss this place—even though it's off the main highways, it's a real treat to visit.

East of Willakenzie in the area known as Ribbon Ridge are a number of mostly small wineries. These back roads, which lie north and west of Newberg, are home to some of Oregon's finest wineries. **Beaux Frères** (15155 NE North Valley Rd., 503/537-1137, open only by appointment and on Memorial Day and Thanksgiving weekends), an old pig farm that has been transformed into a top-notch winery, is partially owned by *Wine Advocate* author and publisher Robert Parker (no, he doesn't rate his own wines). **Patricia Green Cellars** (15225 NE North Valley Rd., 503/554-0821, open Memorial Day and Thanksgiving weekends, at other times call ahead for an appointment) is another small, very well respected winery specializing in pinot noir and sauvignon blanc.

Newberg

Adelsheim (16800 NE Calkins Lane, 503/538-3652), founded in 1971, was one of the first Willamette Valley wineries. From their lovely setting on the slopes of the Chehalem Mountains, the Adelsheims have continued to produce good wine.

Another family-owned winery, **Penner-Ash Wine Cellars** (15771 NE Ribbon Ridge Rd., 503/554-5545, Thurs.–Sun.), is typical of the small quality-driven pinot wineries.

Two miles east of Newberg, **Rex Hill Vineyards** (30835 Rte. 99W, 800/739-4455) highlights pinot noir, pinot gris, chardonnay, and Riesling. Persian rugs, antiques, an ornately carved front door, and a lit fireplace extend a warm welcome to visitors. In warm weather, the garden beckons. Try the winery's excellent pinot gris.

Dundee

At one time, Dundee was known mostly for its filberts (known to most of the world as hazelnuts) and the roadside Dundee Nut House. Now the town has several good restaurants and a plethora of wineries in the hills above town. But drive around; you'll still see filbert orchards.

One of Oregon's largest and oldest (dating from 1967) wineries is **Erath** (9409 NE Worden Hill Rd., 503/538-3318), which in 2006 was purchased by Washington's largest winery, Chateau Ste. Michelle. Erath's wood-paneled tasting room sits high in the Red Hills of Dundee, where beautiful picnic sites command an imposing view of local vineyards and the Willamette Valley. To get there, go 2 miles north from the center of Dundee until you see a blue state highway sign marking the turnoff near the junction of Route 99W and 9th Street. Ninth Street turns into Worden Hill Road, a thoroughfare that's more or less the glory road of Oregon wine. Appropriately, the road looks out over vistas dominated by grapevines.

Close by is **Lange Estate Winery and Vineyards** (18380 NE Buena Vista Dr., 503/538-6476), a good place to try pinot noir, chardonnay, or pinot gris. Oregon-style pinot gris is medium-bodied, bright, and acidic, with citrusy overtone—really good with grilled salmon.

An easy stop on Route 99W east of Dundee is **Duck Pond Cellars** (23145 Rte. 99W, 503/538-3199), which produces wines from both Oregon- and Washington-grown grapes. If you're a price-driven wine shopper, note that this is the place to pick up some less-expensive (but still quite drinkable) wine.

The intersection of Sokol Blosser Lane and Route 99W sits about 2 miles west of Dundee. Sokol Blosser Lane leads to **Sokol Blosser Winery** (5000 Sokol Blosser Lane, 800/582-6688). In addition to its pinot noir, the chardonnay is especially recommended at the tasting room. Also good is the rosé of pinot noir—don't turn up your nose at this pink wine; it's fruity and floral, but not overly sweet.

Located in an old farmhouse in downtown Dundee, the **Argyle Winery** (691 Rte. 99W, 503/538-8520) tasting room is the place to come to sample sparkling wine good enough to have graced the Clintons' White House table (and a certain travel writer's wedding reception). It is the state's leading producer of sparkling wine in the tradition of French champagne.

Domaine Drouhin (6750 Breyman Orchards Rd., 503/864-2700, 11 A.M.–4 P.M. Wed.–Sun.), also near Dundee, is the Oregon outpost of France's famed Drouhin family, and makes excellent pinot noirs in the Burgundy style.

While cruising the wine country, antiques collectors can pull off Route 99 into the town of Lafayette to visit **Lafayette Schoolhouse Antiques** (748 Rte. 99W, 503/864-2720, 10 A.M.–5 P.M. daily), where Oregon's largest antiques display can be found in the old schoolhouse, mill, and auditorium. Imagine 10,000 square feet of antiques spread over three floors in a 1910 building. The mall promises it won't sell reproductions.

◖ Carlton

From Route 99W, jog north on Route 47 to the small town of Carlton, where the **Carlton Winemaker's Studio** (801 N. Scott St., 503/852-6100, www.winemakersstudio.com, June–Sept.) houses several boutique wineries, including Andrew Rich, Hamacher, and Bryce. One purpose of the studio is to help up-and-coming winemakers by providing space and support; several winemakers—including Penner-Ash, Domaine Meriwether, and Scott Paul—have "graduated" to their own facilities.

Right in the heart of tiny downtown Carlton, **The Tasting Room** (105 W. Main St., 503/852-6733, Thurs.–Mon.) sells the bottles of a wide variety of local producers, many of whom run small wineries without formal tasting rooms. Another good place to stop in Carlton during the Memorial Day and Thanksgiving weekends is **Ken Wright Cellars** (236 N. Kutch St., 503/852-7070, www.kenwrightcellars.com), another high-quality winery with chardonnay and pinot blanc in addition to the pinot noir; at other times of year, the Tasting Room represents Wright's wines.

Check out the beautiful facility and one of the most panoramic views in the valley at **Anne**

Amie Vineyards (6580 NE Mineral Springs Rd., 503/864-2991), where you'll also find top-notch pinot noir, pinot blanc, and pinot gris.

McMinnville

The tasting room of **Yamhill Valley Vineyards** (16250 Oldsville Rd., off Rte. 18, 503/843-3100 or 800/825-4845, daily Memorial Day weekend–mid-Dec.) is set amid an oak grove on a 200-acre estate and features a balcony overlooking the vineyard. This winery's first release, an '83 pinot noir, first distinguished itself at a 1985 tasting of French and Oregon vintages held in New York City. Since the 1980s, the winery has maintained this standard.

More than almost any other winemaker, David Lett of **The Eyrie Vineyards** (935 E. 10th St., 503/472-6315, Memorial Day and Thanksgiving weekends only) is responsible for shepherding Oregon's fledgling wine industry. Eyrie started up in 1966 and produced the Willamette Valley's first pinot noir and chardonnay as well as the first pinot gris in the United States. The winery, in an unmarked building on the edge of downtown McMinnville, is usually closed to visitors, but you can taste their wine at most area restaurants.

Step away from the tasting room and into the giant hangars of the **Evergreen Aviation Museum** (500 NE Captain Michael King Smith Way, 503/434-4180, www.sprucegoose.org, 9 A.M.–5 P.M. daily, basic admission to one museum $14 adults, $13 seniors and veterans, $12 students), just off Route 18 south of McMinnville. There are actually two separate museums: an aviation museum and a space museum. Additionally, there's an IMAX theater. You can spend as much as $32 and five hours visiting both museums and taking in an IMAX movie, but many visitors focus just on the original aviation museum, which houses the Spruce Goose, the giant wooden seaplane built for billionaire Howard Hughes in the 1940s. The plane, which Hughes called a "flying boat," flew only once for approximately one minute. In addition to the Goose, the museum houses many other aircraft, including really funky little hand-built planes, bombers, and large cargo planes.

Amity

A classic Yamhill County winery is **Amity Vineyards** (18150 Amity Vineyards Rd. SE, 503/835-2362 or 888/264-8966). The tasting room is located in a huge old barn on a 500-foot hill looking out over southern Yamhill County to the Coast Range, making for some beautiful sunset views. Amity, which was founded in 1974, is one of Oregon's oldest wineries and still has a homespun feel that belies its excellent wines.

The nearby **Kristin Hill Winery** (3330 SE Amity Dayton Hwy., 503/835-0850, Mar.–Dec.) specializes in a traditional "Methode Champenoise" (sparkling wine). Picnickers are welcome.

Amity wines are also featured at the **Lawrence Gallery** (19700 SW Hwy. 18, 503/843-3633) in Sheridan, 9 miles southwest of McMinnville on Route 18. Several dozen other Oregon wines are featured, as well as the work of a multitude of Oregon artists and craftspeople. Five acres of sweeping lawns and gardens surrounding this renovated century-old building make it even more of a reason to stop. Outdoor art pieces proliferate in these elegant landscapes at every turn. Also on-site is the Fresh Palate Cafe, open daily for wine-friendly lunches and Sunday brunch.

Not far from Amity is the monastery of the **Brigittine monks** (23300 Walker Lane, 503/835-8080). Their chocolate truffles and fudge are highly regarded, and the monks rent out rooms for spiritual retreats.

ACCOMMODATIONS

Given the proximity of Portland, most folks do the wine country as a day trip. Should you care to extend your stay, there are plenty of bed-and-breakfasts and a smattering of hotels, including a luxurious resort, to accommodate you.

McMenamins' ◖ **Hotel Oregon** (310 NE Evans St., McMinnville, 800/472-8427, www.mcmenamins.com, $60 and up) has the spirit of fun, good food and drink, and art of the other outposts of the Brothers McMenamin empire. An outdoor rooftop bar, comfy (but not exactly posh) guest rooms (some with private bath, some with shared bath down the hall), and a sumptuous included breakfast make this a winner. For good dollar value, ask about wine-country packages that include a tour of vineyards and meals along with bed and board.

A standard hotel that's a good bet if you're traveling with a dog is the **Comfort Inn** (2520 SE Stratus Ave., McMinnville, 503/472-1700, www.choicehotels.com, $114 and up).

A considerably more posh place to stay outside McMinnville is the **Youngberg Hill Vineyards and Inn** (10660 SW Youngberg Hill Rd., McMinnville, 503/472-2727 or 888/657-8668, www.youngberghill.com, $180 and up), located on a 20-year-old organic vineyard with excellent views of the grapes and the Coast Range, Mount Jefferson, Mount Hood, or the Willamette Valley from the rooms or from the covered decks that surround the inn.

In downtown Carlton, it's a short walk from the **Carlton Inn** (648 W. Main St., 503/852-7506, www.thecarltoninn.com, $125 and up) to tasting rooms and restaurants. There's a touch of Scandinavian cheery color at this friendly B&B. Three of the four guest rooms share a bath; one has a private bath.

Just east of Carlton, the **Lobenhaus B&B** (6975 NE Abbey Rd., Carlton, 503/864-9173 or 888/339-3375, www.lobenhaus.com, $160 and up) is a tri-level lodge on 27 acres with comfortable accommodations and a peaceful atmosphere. Each guest room has a private bath and a deck overlooking a spring-fed pond. Guests can take advantage of two common living rooms, each with a TV and a fireplace.

Nearby, the **Abbey Road Farm B&B** (10501 NE Abbey Rd., Carlton, 503/852-6278, www.abbeyroadfarm.com, $210) has elegant rooms located in (no joke) converted grain silos. This upscale B&B is very nicely appointed; the 82-acre Abbey Road Farm has cherry orchards, goats, llamas, donkeys, and gardens; guests can ask about helping out with farm chores.

Just up the road from Sokol Blosser, **Wine**

Country Farm Cellars (6855 Breyman Orchards Rd., Dayton, 503/864-3446 or 800/261-3446, www.winecountryfarm.com, $150 and up) combines wine growing with bed-and-breakfast accommodations. Watch the pinot noir grow, take a hike, get a massage, or take a trail ride on the resident horses. Guest rooms all have private baths and Wi-Fi.

Although it's right on busy U.S. 99 in Dundee, the 20-room **Inn at Red Hills** (1410 N. Hwy. 99W, 503/538-7666, www.innatredhills.com, $195 and up), a newer boutique hotel, is a gracious and relaxing place to stay, with a good restaurant downstairs and other excellent dining choices right in town.

The wine country's newest and most opulent place to stay is also its only full-on resort, the **Allison Inn** (2525 Allison Lane, Newberg, 503/554-2525 or 877/294-2525, www.theallison.com, $295 and up). Each spacious guest room has a gas fireplace, a soaking tub, a large flat-screen TV, bay window seats, a private terrace or balcony, and just-so furnishings and art. Guests have access to a spa and fitness center with an indoor pool and some rather high-end fitness equipment.

At the other end of the spectrum, the **Flying M Ranch** (23029 NW Flying M Rd., Yamhill, 503/662-3222, www.flying-m-ranch.com, $17 camping, $25 cabin) is more "Western" than wine-snob. Here you can stay in a tiny rustic camping cabin or in your own tent or RV. Sites are nestled in the woods, many with decks overlooking the Yamhill River. Explore the area either on foot or on horseback; the ranch's horses head out on the trails several times a day.

FOOD

As the wine industry has flourished in the northern Willamette Valley, the restaurant scene has developed to keep pace. There used to be one clearly excellent restaurant in the area: Nick's. Now wine-country residents and travelers can pick from a number of good places to eat.

The low-key atmosphere of McMinnville's downtown and the 1950s feel of **Nick's Italian Cafe** (521 3rd St., McMinnville, 503/434-4471, 11 A.M.–2 P.M. and 5:30 P.M.–closing Tues.–Sat., 11:30 A.M.–6:30 P.M. Sun., $49 prix-fixe dinner), a onetime soda fountain, might at first make you wonder whether it's worth stopping by, but Nick's is a wine-country classic with a wine list that is both extensive and distinctive. As host to many wine-country functions, Nick is privy to special releases found nowhere else. The latter are fitting accompaniments to such culinary interpretations as lasagna with Dungeness crab and pine nuts, or rabbit braised in Oregon pinot gris and rosemary with Gorgonzola polenta. The five-course fixed-price dinner is highly recommended; if that isn't in the budget, stop by for a panini sandwich or a wood-fired pizza at lunch ($9–12) or visit the back room in the evening to snack from the bar menu.

Another gem of a restaurant, **Tina's** (760 Rte. 99W, Dundee, 503/538-8880, 11 A.M.–2 P.M. and 5 P.M.–closing Tues.–Sat., 5 P.M.–closing Sun.–Mon., $22–36) is right on busy U.S. 99 in Dundee; as you're heading west, look for a small red boxlike structure on the right-hand side of the road across from the Dundee fire station. Tina's uses the freshest Oregon ingredients to create simple yet elegant fare. This place is a gem, as one bite of the pan-fried oysters will tell you. In what can only be interpreted as a good sign, it's not uncommon to see local winemakers hanging out at the tiny bar.

Just east, where Route 99 meets 7th Street, **Your Northwest** (110 SW 7th St., 503/554-8101) is a complex selling a good selection of indigenous Northwest food and crafts. The venerated **Ponzi Vineyards** has a tasting room here (its main tasting room is in Beaverton) and the **Dundee Bistro** (503/554-1650, 11 A.M.–closing daily, lunch $11–16, dinner $12–22) is a reliable always-open spot for lunch or dinner that's not quite as expensive as some of the more swanky places in the area.

Red Hills Provincial Dining (276 Rte. 99W, Dundee, 503/538-8224, 5–9 P.M. Tues.–Sun., $25–32) is a cozy, charm-filled restaurant that uses only the freshest local ingredients to create award-winning French- and Italian-inspired food.

Also in Dundee is **Farm to Fork** (1410 N. Hwy. 99W, 503/538-7970, 7 A.M.–closing daily, $11–20), one of the area's newer restaurants, which celebrates the chef's relationships with local farmers, foragers, ranchers, and fishermen. Along with its restaurant operations, Farm to Fork offers prepared food to go. It's also one of the few places in the area that's open for breakfast, and it's certainly the best place in Dundee for a breakfast of duck confit hash ($12). Find it inside the Inn at Red Hills.

In Carlton, a good place to sit down to a dinner of country-style French food is **Cuvée** (214 W. Main St., 503/852-6555, 5:30–9:30 P.M. Wed.–Sat., 5–8 P.M. Sun., noon–3 P.M. Sat.–Sun. summer, $21–23). Order French standards such as coquilles St. Jacques, and make sure to check out the sautéed oysters with horseradish sauce as an appetizer. Three-course fixed-price dinners ($25, reservations recommended) are offered Wednesday, Thursday, and Sunday nights.

The 【 **Joel Palmer House** (600 Ferry St., Dayton, 503/864-2995, www.joelpalmerhouse.com, 6–9 P.M. Tues.–Sat., $29–37, reservations recommended) is considered one of Oregon's finest historic homes and is on both the Oregon and the National Historic Registers. It was originally owned by the eponymous Joel Palmer, who was speaker of the Oregon House of Representatives in 1862 and Oregon state senator 1864–1866. Jack and Heidi Czarnecki have turned the Joel Palmer House into a one-of-a-kind restaurant that combines their love of mushroom hunting with fine wine. Many dishes include wild mushrooms, and unless you're really phobic about fungi, they're highly recommended. Indulge your passion for mushrooms with the $75 seven-course mushroom madness dinner

(must be ordered by everyone at your table). The restaurant is located at the junction of Routes 221 and 223, off Route 18.

INFORMATION AND SERVICES

Willamette Valley Wineries (503/646-2985, www.willamettewines.com) maintains an excellent website. Contact the **McMinnville Chamber of Commerce** (417 NW Adams St., McMinnville 97128, 503/538-2014, www.mcminnville.org) or the **Yamhill Valley Visitors Association** (503/883-7770, www.yamhillvalley.org) for winery and accommodations information.

If you prefer to leave the driving and commentary to someone else, several companies offer tours by bus or car, particularly for parties of four or more. Prices vary widely depending on the number of people, the amount of customization, and whether or not meals are provided: a full-day tour can range $60–150 per person; half-day tours are also available. Besides the obvious advantage of being able to swallow rather than spitting, traveling with one of these groups can gain you access to small wineries without regular tasting-room hours. One particularly well-established company is **Grape Escape Winery Tours** (503/283-3380, www.grapeescapetours.com). Tours are also provided by **Eco Tours of Oregon** (503/245-1428, www.ecotours-of-oregon.com), **Insiders Wine Tour** (503/791-0005, www.insiderswinetour.com), and **Eco-Wine Tours** (503/863-7777, www.eco-winetours.com), which specializes in the valley's many wineries with environmentally sustainable practices.

Want to see the valley from a hot-air balloon? Get in touch with the folks at **Vista Balloons** (503/625-7385 or 800/622-2309, www.vistaballoon.com, Apr.–Oct., $189).

Northeastern Willamette Valley

Much of Oregon's early history played out near the banks of the Willamette River between present-day Portland and Salem. Settlers made a break from the British Hudson's Bay Company and established a pro-American provisional government. The fertile land was also the destination of Oregon Trail pioneers. Over 150 years later these Willamette Valley towns are still mostly small, and the surrounding countryside is lush, inviting a ramble through history.

CHAMPOEG STATE PARK

Below Yamhill County, just southeast of Newberg on Route 219, is Champoeg (pronounced sham-POO-ee or sham-POO-eck), often touted as the birthplace of Oregon. The name means "field of roots" in Chinook, referring to the camas coveted by Native Americans, who boiled it to accompany the traditional salmon feast.

Champoeg State Heritage Area (503/678-1251, visitors center 9 A.M.–5 P.M. daily, $3 day-use fee) commemorates the site of the 1843 vote to break free from British and Hudson's Bay Company rule and establish a pro-American provisional government in the Oregon country. To get there from Portland, drive south on I-5 until you see signs for Exit 278. This exit directs you to a rural route that runs 5 miles to the park visitors center. The 568-acre park is equidistant from Portland and Salem along the Willamette River.

The visitors center has exhibits detailing how the Kalapuyas, explorers, French Canadian fur traders, and American settlers lived in the Willamette Valley. The grounds also contain several historic buildings. Adjacent to the visitors center is the Manson Barn, built in 1862. The Old Butteville jail (1850) and one-room schoolhouse have also been moved to Champoeg to help evoke frontier life. Just west

The Willamette River runs through Champoeg State Park.

© JUDY JEWELL

of the park entrance is a replica of the 1852 house of pioneer Robert Newell (503/678-5537, 1–5 P.M. Fri.–Sun. Mar.–Oct.). Particularly interesting is the second floor, which showcases Native American artifacts and a collection of inaugural gowns worn by the wives of Oregon governors. The **Pioneer Mother's Museum** replicates the dwellings in the Willamette Valley circa 1850. A collection of 1775–1850 guns and muskets is also on display. Besides the historical exhibits, Champoeg features a botanical garden of native plants as well as hiking and biking trails.

If you want to extend your stay, Champoeg State Park offers six tent sites and 48 sites with RV hookups ($19 tents, $24 RVs). There are also six yurts for rent ($27). Call 800/452-5687 for reservations ($8 reservation fee). This year-round facility is one of the few out-of-town campgrounds within easy driving distance (25 miles) of Portland. Add beautiful Willamette River frontage and prime bike-riding on the nearby country roads, and you might consider this the consummate budget alternative to a night in the city or a pricey wine-country B&B.

Willamette Mission State Park is also in this area (just look for signs). It is home to one of the world's largest cottonwoods and the charming Wheatland car ferry across the Willamette River.

FRENCH PRAIRIE LOOP

Before leaving Champoeg State Park, pick up a brochure at the visitors center outlining the French Prairie Loop, a 40-mile byway for car and bicycle touring. History buffs, thrift shoppers, and antique aficionados will enjoy the chance to indulge their passions along this route. French Canadian trappers settled here in the 1820s and 1830s to help the Hudson's Bay Company establish a presence in the Willamette Valley. During the 1849 California gold rush, wheat and produce from this area were shipped to granaries and warehouses in the area of present-day Portland and on to San Francisco.

Churches and buildings dating back to the 19th century have earned **St. Paul,** one of the towns on the loop (Rte. 219), National Historic District status. The Northwest's oldest Catholic church, St. Paul's, dates to circa 1846; some parishioners claim ancestral links with the French Canadian trappers who were Oregon's first permanent white settlers. The building underwent a $1 million reconstruction after being damaged by an earthquake in 1993. The church was rebuilt with its original bricks and was reinforced with concrete. Each Fourth of July weekend, an Oregon tradition takes place with the flat-out fun **St. Paul Rodeo** (800/237-5920, www.stpaulrodeo.com), which includes a fireworks display, a barbecue, and an art auction. The prize money is good, so you'll see many top riders and ropers competing.

On the east side of the loop, **Aurora,** at the junction of Routes 219 and 99, also enjoys National Historic District status. Oregon's legacy as a haven for utopian communities began here with a Prussian immigrant, Dr. William Keil. He started a communal colony for Oregon Trail pioneers, naming the town that grew out of it after his daughter. The Aurora colony fused Christian fundamentalism with collectivist principles, garnering distinction for its thriving farms and the excellence of its handicrafts. Despite Aurora's early success, a smallpox epidemic in 1862 and the coming of the railroad, which undermined Willamette River trade in the subsequent decade, provided the catalysts for the town's demise. Keil himself died in 1877, and the struggling colony disbanded a few years later.

The **Old Aurora Colony Museum** (15018 2nd St. NE, Aurora, 503/678-5754, 11 A.M.–4 P.M. Tues.–Sat., noon–4 P.M. Sun. Feb.–Dec., $6 adults, $5 seniors, $2 students) consists of five buildings, including two of the colony's homesteads, the communal washhouse, and the farm equipment shed. Items of interest include old tools, a collection of musical instruments, and a recording left over from the colony band, as well as quilts and an herb garden.

The museum is easily located by turning east as you enter town. After one block you'll see the museum, housed in a former ox barn. Sometimes colony descendants are on hand to answer questions or demonstrate historical objects such as an ingenious spinning wheel devised by William Keil. After visiting the museum, you can take an Aurora walking tour (ask for the free pamphlet) of 33 nearby structures such as clapboard and Victorian houses as well as antique shops, all clustered along Route 99E.

OREGON CITY

North of Canby, Route 99E attractively parallels the Willamette River. Jagged rock bluffs on one side of the highway contrast with the smooth-flowing river framed by stately cottonwood and poplar trees. More variety is added by islands in the channel and the broad expanse of 40-foot **Willamette Falls** in Oregon City. As the terminus of the Oregon Trail and the only seat of American power in the territory until 1852, this town is the site of many firsts. Leading off the list is Oregon City's status as the first incorporated city west of the Rockies. Other claims to fame include the West's first mint, paper mill, and newspaper, and the world's first long-distance electric power transmission system. The Oregon territorial capital was also the site of the state's first Protestant church and Masonic lodge.

Ironically, a representative of British interests in Oregon country is credited with starting Oregon City. John McLoughlin, the Canadian-born chief factor of the Hudson's Bay Company, encouraged French Canadian trappers to cross the Columbia River from Fort Vancouver and settle here in the northern Willamette Valley, inspiring the name French Prairie. To further the development of this British beachhead, McLoughlin built a flour mill near Willamette Falls in 1832. He moved down to Oregon City himself in the 1840s and became an ardent supporter of American settlers who wanted Oregon to be independent of England and part of the United States.

McLoughlin's flour mill set the precedent for other uses of water power. It also helped attract pioneers who came over the Cascades via the Barlow Road extension of the Oregon Trail. As a result, Oregon City became a manufacturing center. Its river port thrived due to Willamette Falls impeding the movement of merchant ships farther south on the river. Although the development of the railroad and the city of Portland diminished Oregon City's importance, its glory days live on today thanks to National Historic District status. Buildings that date back to the mid-19th century exemplify Queen Anne, Federal, and Italianate architectural styles.

Basalt terraces divide the city into three levels. Downtown is wedged between the river and a 100-foot bluff. A municipal elevator provides transportation between the commercial traffic in the lower part of town and historic building on the bluff. Years ago, the McLoughlin House was originally situated on the river but later was moved to the heights to make room for "progress."

Museum of the Oregon Territory

Heading north on Route 99E from Willamette Falls, look for the Tumwater turnoff on the east side of the highway for the Museum of the Oregon Territory (211 Tumwater Dr., 503/655-5574, 11 A.M.–4 P.M. Tues.–Sat., $9 adults, $7 seniors, $5 children). From the elevated perspective of the museum parking lot you'll have a great bird's-eye view of Willamette Falls. Prior to perusing the diaries, artifacts, and historic photos on the second floor, you'll encounter a timeline that correlates world events over thousands of years to the geologic, political, and social growth of Oregon. This imparts a larger perspective to what you'll see in the exhibit hall. Signposts for your journey through the ages include Native American baskets and arrowheads, a horse-drawn carriage, and the world's first kidney dialysis machine (invented locally). The county collection serves as a valuable complement to the End of the Trail Interpretive Center and historic homes just north of here, and one admission fee gets you into most of these places.

McLoughlin House

For a glimpse of the glory that was 19th-century Oregon City, take a right turn (east) off Route 99E (McLoughlin Blvd.) onto 7th Street and follow it to the base of the cliff. At 7th and Railroad Streets, you'll see an immense gray elevator (7 A.M.–7 P.M. Mon.–Sat., free) scaling the 90-foot escarpment rising up from the lower section of town. Take a left turn when you exit the elevator, and a few minutes' stroll northeast along the cliff top will have you peering across a street at the back yard of an Oregon City landmark.

The McLoughlin House (713 Center St. between 7th St. and 8th St., 503/656-5146, 10 A.M.–4 P.M. Wed.–Sat., 1–4 P.M. Sun., closed mid-Dec.–Jan. 31, free, subject to change) is an impressive clapboard-style home of the "Father of Oregon." To spare it flood damage, the building was moved from its original site near the river to this location. Behind it are steps leading back to the lower section of town. The collection of original and period furnishings may not be terribly exciting, but the rangers' ghost stories and historical insights can make it all come alive. In addition, the grounds are lovingly landscaped with rhododendrons, azaleas, and roses. The McLoughlin House is actually a national park site that is part of Fort Vancouver, just across the Columbia River in Washington.

End of the Trail Interpretive Center

The End of the Trail Interpretive Center (1726 Washington St., 503/657-0988, www.endoftheoregontrail.org, 9:30 A.M.–5 P.M. Mon.–Sat., 10:30 A.M.–5 P.M. Sun., $9 adults, $7 seniors, $5 children, includes admission to Museum of the Oregon Territory) showcases Oregon City's claim as the terminus of the Oregon Trail. This status is also claimed by The Dalles, a city in the Columbia River Gorge. Without belaboring the merits of each claim, suffice it to say that Oregon City was at the end of the Barlow Trail, a spur route over Mount Hood from The Dalles for pioneers understandably leery of the raft trip down the Columbia River.

This large interpretive center was built to commemorate the 150th anniversary of the Great Migration of 1843. To get there coming from Portland, take I-205 south to the Park Place Exit, turn south on Route 213, and follow the signs to Abernethy Green. Organizers have selected an area often identified as the end of the Barlow Road section of the trail to set up these facilities. To find them, follow Washington Street north to its intersection with Abernethy Road, or ask one of the locals for directions to Kelly Field. From I-205, you should be able to see three connected buildings in the shape of giant covered wagons.

John Inskeep Environmental Learning Center

The John Inskeep Environmental Learning Center (Clackamas Community College, 19600 Molalla Ave., 503/657-6958, ext. 2351, dawn–dusk daily, $2), 3 miles north of Kelly Field on Route 213, is pioneering efforts of a different sort. The 80-acre environmental-study area showcases alternative technologies and recycling against a backdrop of ponds, trails, and wildlife. Exhibits on aquaculture, birds of prey, and wetlands are included in this environmental education center's portrayal of Oregon's ecosystems. The exhibits are supplemented by one of the largest telescopes in the Northwest (503/657-6958, ext. 5665, open on clear nights when a volunteer is available, $3, call to confirm). Adjacent to the Inskeep Environmental Learning Center is the **Home Orchard Society Arboretum,** displaying Oregon's array of fruit-bearing plants.

Information

If you're exploring Oregon City and need a map, you can get one in the municipal elevator. There's also a **State Welcome Center** at 1726 Washington Street (503/657-9336, ext. 114, or 800/424-3002).

Salem

The used-car lots and fast-food outlets encountered on the way into Salem off I-5 contrast with the inspiring murals and displays in the capitol, where it is comforting to be reminded of Oregon's pioneer tradition and proud legacy of progressive legislation. Close by, the tranquil beauty and stimulating museums of historic Willamette University also provide a break from the carbon-copy drabness of a town dominated by gray buildings housing the state's bureaucracies.

The Kalapuyan name for the locality of Salem was Chemeketa, or "Place of Rest." Connotations of repose were also captured by the Methodist missionary name Salem, an anglicized form of the Arabic *salaam* and the Hebrew *shalom*, meaning "peace." The surrounding croplands along with Willamette River transport and waterpower quickly enabled Salem to become the New Jerusalem envisioned by Oregon Trail pioneers. Over the years, the city forged an economic destiny in government, food processing, light manufacturing, and wood products. Today, it has a population of about 153,000.

SIGHTS
◖ State Capitol
If visiting the State Capitol (900 NE Court St., 503/986-1388, 9 A.M.–4 P.M. Mon.–Fri., free) strikes you as the kind of saccharine excursion best reserved for a first-grade class trip, you're in for a pleasant surprise. The marble halls of Oregon government are adorned with attractive murals, paintings, and sculptures of the seminal events in the state's history. The capitol is located on Court Street between West Summer and East Summer Streets, just north of Willamette University.

Atop the capitol dome is a gold-leafed bronze statue of a bearded ax-wielding pioneer. Massive marble sculptures flank the main entrance—*Covered Wagons* on the west side and *Lewis and Clark Led by Sacagawea* on the east. Maps of the Oregon Trail and the

The Oregon State Capitol is topped with a gold-leafed statue of a pioneer.

route of Lewis and Clark are visible on the backs of the statues. The symbolism is sustained after you enter the double glass doors to the rotunda. Your eyes will immediately be drawn to a bronze state seal, eight feet in diameter and set into the floor, that juxtaposes an eagle in flight, a sailing ship, a covered wagon, and forests. The 33 marble steps beyond the cordoned-off emblem lead up to the House and Senate chambers and symbolize Oregon's place as the 33rd state to enter the Union. Four large murals adorning the rose travertine walls of the rotunda illustrate the settlement and growth of Oregon: Robert Gray sailing into the Columbia estuary in 1792; Lewis and Clark at Celilo Falls in 1805; the first white women to cross the continent being welcomed by Dr. John McLoughlin in 1836; and the first wagon train on the Oregon Trail in 1843. Bronze reliefs and smaller murals symbolic of Oregon's

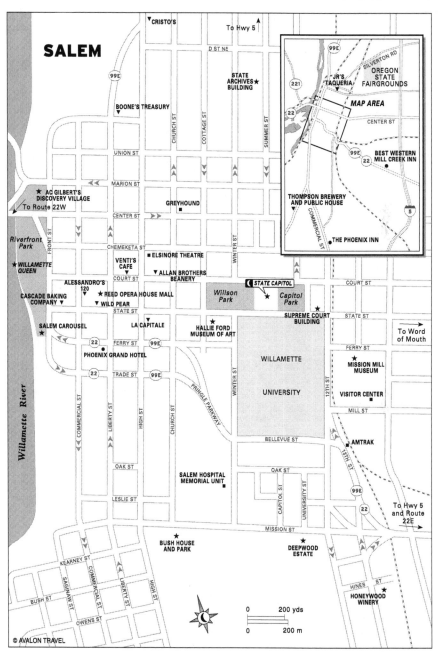

ENCHANTED FOREST

Seven miles south of Salem off I-5 on Exit 248 is the Enchanted Forest (8462 Enchanted Way, Turner, 503/371-4262, www.enchantedforest. com), one man's answer to Walt Disney. An enterprising Oregonian has single-handedly built a false-front Western town, a haunted house, and many more attractions.

In the 1960s Roger Tofte, the father of four young children, realized there was very little for a family to see and do together in Salem. He formulated the idea for a theme park where he could use his creative talents. Although he had very little time or money to make his dream a reality, he was able to purchase the original 20 acres of land off I-5 for $4,000 in monthly payments of $50. In 1964 he began construction.

Finally, in 1971, Tofte officially opened the park. Over the years, Tofte has successfully incorporated three of his children into the business: Susan (co-operations officer and artistic director), Mary (co-operations of-ficer and chief financial officer), and Ken (head of attractions development and ride maintenance).

Whether it's the old woman who lived in the shoe, the seven dwarves' cottage, or Alice in Wonderland's rabbit hole, these and other nursery-rhyme and fairy-tale re-creations will get a thumbs-up from anyone under 99 years of age. One of the most inventive attractions is an old English village that features a life-sized Geppetto and Pinocchio telling stories punctuated by animated characters popping their heads out of windows.

The park has a few schedule quirks; it's best to check the website if you are going to be visiting 5-6 P.M. Basically, it is open 10 A.M.-5 or 6 P.M. daily March 15-March 31; weekends only in April; daily May-Labor Day; weekends only in September; closed October-March 15th. Admission is $9.95 for adults, $8.95 for seniors and kids ages 3-12, $0.80 extra for some rides.

industries also are displayed. The best part of the capitol is the legislative chambers, up the sweeping marble staircases.

Near the ceiling in the Senate and House chambers are friezes depicting an honor roll of people who influenced the growth and settlement of Oregon. Included are Thomas Jefferson, who sanctioned the Lewis and Clark expedition, and Thomas Condon, native son and naturalist extraordinaire. Also among the names are those of six women, headed by Lewis and Clark's interpreter-guide Sacagawea. The biggest surprise in the array might be John Quincy Adams, who determined the southern boundary of Oregon when he was secretary of state. In both legislative chambers look for forestry, agricultural, and fishing symbols woven into the carpets; murals about the coming of statehood are behind the speakers' rostrums.

Among the many architecturally eye-catching features to be found in the capitol are the rotunda's black marble, the House chamber walls and furnishings of golden oak, black walnut room appointments in the Senate, a walnut-paneled governor's office, and bronze doorknobs inlaid with the state seal throughout the building. There is also a carved myrtlewood table inlaid with a mosaic of the capitol in the reception area outside the governor's suite between the House and the Senate. All this was paid for with part of the $2 million it took to build the capitol in 1938.

If you don't want to roam independently, free half-hour building tours are given on the hour 9 A.M.-4 P.M. weekdays, with a lunch break noon-1 P.M.

A tower at the top of the capitol building gives a superlative view of the valley and surrounding Cascade peaks, worth the 121-step climb from the fourth floor. It's open Memorial Day-September (but closes when the temperature reaches 90°F) and other times of the year by appointment; call 541/986-1388 for tour information. Also worth a look is the ongoing exhibit of outstanding Oregon artists in the governor's ceremonial office upstairs. Downstairs is a fine gift shop and a café. On the west side of the building (Court St. entrance) is an indoor visitors information kiosk.

To get to the Oregon State Capitol from I-5, take Exit 253 to Route 22 West. Take the Willamette University/State Offices Exit and follow the signs for 12th Street/State Offices. Turn left onto Court Street.

State Archives Building

Just north of the Capitol Mall, the State Archives Building (800 N. Summer St., 503/373-0701, 8 A.M.–noon and 1–4:45 P.M. Mon.–Fri.) is known by some Oregonians mostly for it luxurious interior decor commissioned in an era of belt-tightening. It's worth a look at the art in the building's foyer, but in order to get into the archives area, you'll have to fill out a bit of paperwork stating your research objective. (Saying you are a tourist, we've found, is insufficient.) But the archives do contain the scrawled accounts of a meeting of early state leaders, first-hand descriptions of settler life, and original documents relating to the Oregon Territory as well as the first copy of the state constitution. It's all summed up quite well by the words below a striking glass mural of the pioneers in the reception area: "To think we came all that way, risked everything, used our bodies as plows, and arrived here with our lives."

Capitol Grounds

At each end of the capitol are parks featuring giant sequoias, magnolias, and Camperdown elms. Between the capitol and the state executive building on the corner of Court and Cottage Streets is **Willson Park.** Lush lawns, a gazebo for concerts, and a wide variety of trees, including sequoias, Port Orford cedars, Asian cedars, blue spruces, mountain ashes, dogwoods, and incense cedars, invite a picnic. Two large multicolored rose gardens bloom through much of the year to garnish your spread, and a trio of bronze beavers make the perfect lunch companions. Also to the west of the building are the beautiful E. M. Waite Memorial Fountain and a replica of the Liberty Bell. To the east is **Capitol Park,** where you can admire Corinthian columns salvaged from the old capitol (destroyed by fire in 1935) and statues of Dr. John McLoughlin, Reverend Jason Lee, and the circuit rider, honoring horseback evangelists to the pioneers during the era of missionary zeal.

The oldest government building in Salem is the **Supreme Court building** (1147 State St.), dating back to 1914. It's located to the east of the capitol on the southern half of the block across Waverly Street, facing State Street and bounded by 12th Street. The building's facade is white terra-cotta, and the marble interior has tile flooring. Visual highlights include an ornate stairwell and a stained-glass skylight in the third-floor courtroom framing a replica of the Oregon state seal. Above all, don't miss the public restrooms. Tastefully appointed in marble, oak, and tile, these facilities were described in *Oregon* magazine as "doing justice to public needs."

Willamette University

Just south of the capitol mall is Willamette University (900 State St., 503/370-6300), the oldest institution of higher learning west of the Mississippi. It began as the Oregon Institute in 1842, a school that Methodist missionary Jason Lee founded to instill Christian values among the settlers. Over the years, Willamette University has turned out its share of Oregon politicos, including longtime senators Mark Hatfield and Bob Packwood. It also has to be one of the prettier campuses in the nation.

The campus is one of Salem's many oases of greenery that soften the hard edge of a city dominated by government buildings and nondescript downtown thoroughfares. Campus landscape architecture features a Japanese garden (the Martha Springer Garden, at the southeast corner of campus, also boasts roses, a rock garden, and an English perennial garden), ornate fountains, and a grove of five sequoias six feet in diameter. When you stand in the middle of these redwoods, you should be able to discern a star pattern formed by their canopies, giving rise to the name "star trees." This grove, which sits between the state capitol and Collins Hall, home of the science departments, has beside it an Oregon rock of ages. Found atop Ankeny Hill in Salem, the granite boulder floated down from northeastern Washington on an ice raft during the same Missoula Floods that shaped the Columbia River Gorge eons ago. This glacial erratic stands as a reminder that the Willamette Valley is largely composed of Lake Missoula sediments. In Collins Hall, crystals and exhibits on Oregon glacial activity join an impressive taxidermic array of Oregon wildlife. There's no admission charge, and it's open during university hours. Finally, if you're hungry, the food court at the student union, Goudy Commons, is exceptional, reasonably priced, and with enough variety to suit all tastes.

Hallie Ford Museum of Art

Also part of Willamette University, the Hallie Ford Museum (700 State St., 503/370-6875, 10 A.M.–5 P.M. Tues.–Sat., 1–5 P.M. Sun., $3 adults, $2 students and seniors) features Native American baskets and a third-century Buddhist bas-relief from Pakistan. Asian pieces are also prominent. Contemporary work is exhibited on a rotating basis.

Mission Mill Museum

Just east of Willamette University, a complex of historic buildings along an old millstream make up the Mission Mill Museum (1313 SE Mill St., 503/585-7012, www.missionmill. com, 10 A.M.–5 P.M. Mon.–Sat., $6 adults, $5 seniors, $3 youth 6–17). Its centerpiece is the reconstructed Thomas Kay Woolen Mill. The oldest frame house in the Northwest and water turbines converting fleece into wool fabric are interesting, and the local fiber arts guild uses the building for classes. Several historic homes, including the Jason Lee House and Parsonage, have been moved to this site. The Jason Lee houses, along with the Boon Home, were part of a Methodist mission to the Native Americans. However, those with limited time might prefer to come here just to

obtain brochures about the Salem area at the reception area in front.

The **Marion County Historical Society Museum** (503/364-2128, noon–4 P.M. Tues.–Sat.) is also here, with exhibits on Kalapuyan Indian culture.

To get to the museum from I-5, exit at Route 22, go west on Mission Street for 2 miles to the 13th Street overpass, turn north onto 12th Street, and go west on Mill Street. If you arrive by Amtrak, Mission Mill is within walking distance.

Deepwood Estate

The historic Deepwood Estate (1116 SE Mission St., 503/363-1825, gardens dawn–dusk daily, house tours noon–4 P.M. Sun.–Fri. mid-May–mid-Sept., 11 A.M.–3 P.M. Wed.–Thurs. and Sat. mid-Sept.–mid-May, $4 adults, $3 students and seniors, $2 children) features tours of an elegant 1894 Queen Anne–style home with hand-carved woodwork, gorgeous stained-glass windows, and a well-marked nature trail. English formal gardens here were designed in the 1930s by the Pacific Northwest's first women-owned landscape architecture firm; the Pringle Creek Trail's native flora and the public greenhouse's tropical plants are also worth visiting. Parking is at 12th and Lee Streets near the greenhouse. Sit in Deepwood's pagoda-like gazebo with the scent of boxwood heavy in the air on a spring afternoon and you'll soon forget the hue and cry of political proceedings at the capitol.

Bush House and Park

Bush House Museum (600 Mission St., 503/581-2228, noon–5 P.M. Wed.–Sun. May–Sept., 1–4 P.M. Wed.–Sun. Oct.–Dec. and Mar.–Apr., $4 adults, $3 students and seniors, $2 children 6–12) is located in Bush Pasture Park off Mission, High, and Bush Streets. This 1877 Victorian, with many original furnishings, is the former home of pioneer banker and newspaper publisher Asahel Bush, who once wrote about his competitor, "There's not a brothel in the land that would not have been disgraced by the presence of the

Oregonian." Even if you're not big on house tours, the Italian marble fireplaces and elegant walnut-and-mahogany staircase are worth a look. The house is part of the 80-acre Bush Pasture Park. Besides being a sylvan retreat for picnickers and sports enthusiasts, the park is home to the **Bush Barn Art Center** (541/581-2228, 11 A.M.–6 P.M. Wed.–Fri., noon–5 P.M. Sat.–Sun., free). Located next to the Bush House, this center features two galleries with monthly exhibits. To get there from I-5, take Exit 253 and drive 2 miles west on Route 22 (Mission St.). Turn south on High Street and enter the park on Bush Street, one block south of Madison.

Riverfront Park

Downtown Salem is bordered to the west by the Willamette River, and Riverfront Park is a good place for a stroll, a carousel ride, or a riverboat excursion. The carousel horses (101 Front St. NE, 503/540-9301, www.salemcarousel. org, 10 A.M.–7 P.M. Mon.–Sat., 11 A.M.–6 P.M. Sun. June–Aug., 10 A.M.–6 P.M. Mon.–Thurs., 10 A.M.–7 P.M. Fri.–Sat., 11 A.M.–5 P.M. Sun. Sept.–May, $1.50) were hand-carved by volunteers, and it's no antique; it was built in the late 1990s.

Along the river near the carousel, find the **Willamette Queen** (200 Water St. NE, 503/371-1103, www.willamettequeen.com), a stern-wheeler that cruises the Willamette year-round. Lunch cruises are offered noon–1 P.M. Tuesday–Saturday ($22 adults, $16 children 4–10); one-hour afternoon cruises without food are less expensive (2 P.M., $12 adults, $6 children) and allow you to eat at a good restaurant a short walk away in downtown. Dinner and Sunday brunch cruises are also offered. This is a good way to get a decent look at the river and, if you're lucky, some of its wildlife.

A. C. Gilbert's Discovery Village

Also in Riverfront Park, find A. C. Gilbert's Discovery Village (116 NE Marion St., 503/371-3631 or 800/208-9514, www. acgilbert.org, 10 A.M.–5 P.M. Mon.–Sat., noon–5 P.M. Sun., $5.75, $4.25 seniors, $2.75

toddlers ages 1–2), a cheerful cluster of restored Victorians that also houses the national Toy Hall of Fame. Inspired by A. C. Gilbert, a Salem native whose many inventions included the Gilbert Chemistry Set and the Erector Set, Discovery Village's hands-on expositions incorporate art, music, drama, science, and nature. Whether you're designing a card or bookmark in the craft room, putting on a puppet show, or disassembling a parking meter, the outlets for creativity here are adaptable to any mood or mind-set. If you don't have participatory inclinations, you can still enjoy fascinating exhibits like the one dedicated to A. C. Gilbert, whose Olympian athletic exploits and proficiency as a world-class magician were overshadowed by his inventions. As you might expect, even the gift shop here is a winner.

Honeywood Winery

Of the half-dozen local vintners, Honeywood Winery (1350 Hines St. SE, 503/362-4111, 9 A.M.–5 P.M. Mon.–Fri., 10 A.M.–5 P.M. Sat., 1–5 P.M. Sun.) is the oldest and the most easily reached. It also bills itself as Oregon's oldest winery, having opened in 1933. Honeywood produces a full line of fruit (including Concord grape) and honey wines. Salem's wine country proper is largely clustered along Route 22 (north of the highway) in a region known as the Eola Hills. Ask the folks at the Honeywood tasting room for information.

Reed Opera House Mall

At the corner of Court and Liberty is the Reed Opera House Mall. This onetime venue of minstrel shows and other pioneer cultural activities still retains a brick facade and long windows but has new tenants—the boutiques and restaurants of a tastefully rendered shopping mall.

Gardens

Both **Schreiner's Iris Gardens** (3625 NE Quinaby Rd., 503/393-3232) and **Cooley's Gardens** (11553 NE Silverton Rd., Silverton, 503/873-5463) bill themselves as the world's largest iris growers. Both claims are correct based on different criteria, but the important thing to remember is that from mid-May through the first week of June these are the places to visit to take in the peak blossom seasons. Schreiner's is 7 miles north of Salem next to I-5, and Cooley's is on the way to Silver Falls State Park. Both places can be visited 8 A.M.–dusk.

ENTERTAINMENT AND EVENTS

Salem's recreational mix belies its reputation for being a town dedicated to legislation and little else. The **Elsinore Theatre** (170 High St. SE, 503/375-3574, www.elsinoretheatre.com) is a vintage theater and an emerging downtown cultural venue that features music performances and classic films as well as live theater. Check the *Statesman Journal* for what's scheduled. Along with the L. B. Day amphitheater at the fairgrounds hosting big-name acts and brewpubs featuring live music, there are summer concerts at Salem Riverfront Park.

Bring a real Oregon souvenir home from the state fair – a chainsaw sculpture.

© JUDY JEWELL

Five miles west of downtown, the **Pentacle Theatre** (324 52nd Ave. NW, 503/364-7200, www.pentacletheatre.org) hosts an award-winning eight-play season.

Salem is full of studio tours, downtown art tours, and art galleries, as well as theater and musical events. The Friday *Statesman Journal*'s "Weekend" section gives complete cultural listings.

The Salem Art Association (600 Mission St., 503/581-2228) puts on the **Salem Art Fair and Festival** the third week of July. This multiday event includes 200 artists, performing arts, food, children's activities, a five-kilometer run, an Oregon authors' table, wine and cheese tasting, and art-technique demonstrations.

The **Oregon State Fair** (2330 NE 17th St., 503/947-3247 or 800/833-0011, www. oregonstatefair.org) is an annual celebration held in Salem during the 12 days prior to Labor Day. The fair showcases Oregon agriculture, industries, tourist attractions, natural resources, government, and cultural activities. Big-name entertainment (well, it's actually often big-name has-beens), amusement-park rides, an international photography show, and a horticultural exhibit are also included in this blend of carnival and commerce. The best way to get there off I-5 is via Exits 253 or 258. Admission is $10 for ages 13 and up, $6 for seniors, $5 children 6–12, and children under 5 get in free; save a couple of bucks by buying tickets in advance at Safeway. Parking is $5. Entertainment tickets for musical events can run an extra $5–25. This is the largest agricultural fair on the West Coast. It is also host to one of the 10 largest horse shows in the nation. While there's no shortage of worthwhile events, family fun can come with a hefty price tag.

SPORTS AND RECREATION
Bicycling and Walking

Although Salem is not the cycling paradise that you'll find in nearby Willamette Valley cities of Portland, Eugene, and Corvallis, it is possible to have some fun on two wheels. The

© JUDY JEWELL

An aerial tram runs through the Oregon State Fairgrounds.

best news is the trail through Riverfront Park and the new **Union Street Railroad Bicycle and Pedestrian Bridge** over the Willamette River (previously hard to cross without a car). The bridge links Riverfront Park with Wallace Marine Park on the west side of the river. Another good place to cycle, skate, or walk is **Minto-Brown Island Park** (2200 Minto Island Rd. SE), a large natural park with lots of trails and an off-leash dog park. Find it along the east bank of the Willamette River south of the capitol area.

Golf

The **Salem Golf Club** (2025 Golf Course Rd., 503/363-6652) is one of the best public courses in the state. Another option is **Santiam Golf Course** (8724 Golf Club Rd., Aumsville, 503/769-3485): If you drive 15 minutes east on Route 22 (at Exit 12), you can look forward to combining a round of golf with a walk in the country. Low greens fees and a full-service restaurant and bar add to the pleasure.

ACCOMMODATIONS

Salem has a handful of B&Bs, but its lodgings are largely mid-priced chain hotels clustered east of I-5 at Exit 252 south of downtown. The choice spot to stay is the downtown **C Phoenix Grand Hotel** (201 Liberty St. SE, 503/540-7800 or 877/540-7800, www.phoenixgrandhotel.com, $149 and up), an elegant hotel and conference center with large, nicely furnished guest rooms and a good restaurant. Don't confuse this with the **Phoenix Inn** (4370 Commercial St., 503/588-9220, www.phoenixinnsuites.com, $109 and up) near I-5, which is also an OK place to stay, with "mini-suites" with microwaves and refrigerators as well as access to exercise and spa facilities. Also reasonable is the **Best Western Mill Creek Inn** (3125 Ryan Dr. SE, 503/585-3332 or 800/346-9659, www.bestwestern.com/millcreekinn, $121 and up), with large rooms and a range of amenities comparable to those found at the Phoenix Inn, plus a free shuttle service to the Salem Airport and Amtrak as well as an included breakfast at a nearby Denny's.

If you don't mind staying a little ways north of town, the **Hopewell House B&B** (22350 Hopewell Rd. NW, 503/868-7848, www.hopewellbb.com, $145 and up) is a good place to relax in a newer B&B with lodging in cottages with kitchens, hot tubs, and a rural setting.

If you're looking for more modestly priced accommodations, try the **Travelodge** (1555 State St., 503/581-2466, $62 and up). It's nothing fancy, but it is very clean and convenient.

FOOD

Salem's dining is beginning to rise up from its longtime general mediocrity. Strangely enough, for a city so perfectly situated in Oregon's richest farming country, many places rely on the Sysco truck for their ingredients. But there are exceptions. **C Word of Mouth** (140 17th St. NE, 503/930-4285, 7 A.M.–9 P.M. Mon.–Sat., 8 A.M.–2 P.M. Sun., $10–16), located in an old house east of the capitol and Willamette University, is known for its delicious breakfasts ($4–10), where corned beef hash is the signature dish, but the omelets are also exceptionally good. WOM bills itself as a neighborhood bistro, but Salemites are coming from all over town to eat summertime salads of fresh-picked tomatoes.

A bright spot in downtown Salem is **La Capitale** (508 State St., 503/585-1975, 11 A.M.–9 P.M. Tues.–Fri., noon–9 P.M. Sat., $10–24), where the bistro-style food has a distinct French touch. Even if you're here between meals, nibble on the house-made charcuterie ($10.50) of rosemary-cured ham, thin-sliced pork rillettes, and dry-cured salami. For lunch, the smoked trout and new potato salad is unlike any other lunch you're likely to find in Salem ($8.50).

Another good, and extremely popular, downtown spot is **Wild Pear** (372 State St., 503/378-7515, 10 A.M.–5:30 P.M. Mon.–Sat., $7–13), a lunchtime restaurant and catering business with a good selection of sandwiches and salads. Lunches are large, but you might still consider adding an order of white-truffle sweet potato fries with mustard aioli.

Venti's Cafe (325 Court St. NE, 503/399-8733, 11 A.M.–11 P.M. Mon.–Thurs., 11 A.M.–1 A.M. Fri.–Sat., $6–9) is a little bit Asian and a little bit Mediterranean, with falafels, rice bowls, and wraps, including lots of vegetarian options. It's also a little bit of a club, especially down in the basement, where there's a full bar.

Another downtown place that's good to know about is **Cascade Baking Company** (229 State St., 503/589-0491, 7 A.M.–6 P.M. Mon.–Fri., 9 A.M.–3 P.M. Sat., mini pizza $4), which supplies bread to some of Salem's best restaurants and cooks up a big batch of personal-sized pizzas every day at lunchtime. Panini sandwiches and pastries are also available. This is far and away the best bakery in the area.

If you're looking for a pizza joint, **Christo's** (1108 Broadway NE, 503/371-2892, 11:30 A.M.–2 P.M. and 4:30–8 P.M. Mon.–Thurs., 11:30 A.M.–2 P.M. and 4:30–9 P.M. Fri., 5–9 P.M. Sat., lunch pizzas $5.25–8.50, dinner $12.75–27), in what is beginning to emerge as

a lively neighborhood just north of downtown, is a fun place with good pizza.

There are a couple of **Allan Brothers Beanery** locations in town: one near the government buildings (545 Court St., 503/584-7797, 6 A.M.–6 P.M. Mon.–Fri.) and the other downtown (220 Liberty St. NE, 6 A.M.–9 P.M. Mon.–Fri., 7 A.M.–9 P.M. Sat.–Sun., $4–9). Both have light breakfasts, good homemade pastries, soups, quiche, sandwiches, and deli salads.

Among Salem's many Mexican restaurants, one that stands out is **Jr's Taqueria** (1705 Winter St. NE, 503/378-0500, $2–7), located in a cute little converted gas station. It's a good place for some lunchtime carnitas. Don't worry—even with that name, it's authentic! **Hacienda Real** (475 Taggart Dr. NW, 503/585-3855, 11 A.M.–10 P.M. Mon.–Thurs., 11 A.M.–11 P.M. Fri.–Sat., $7–14), which has a couple of other locations around town, is known for its excellent homemade tortillas and its Jalisco-style food.

Of course, the McMenamins have an outpost in Salem: at **Boon's Treasury** (888 Liberty St. NE, 503/399-9062, 11 A.M.–midnight Mon.–Thurs., 11 A.M.–1 A.M. Fri.–Sat., noon–11 P.M. Sun., $8–13), you can down microbrews and enjoy live music amid the brick confines of the old treasury building or hang out in the backyard beer garden.

Bentley's Grill (291 Liberty St. SE, 503/779-1660, 11 A.M.–10 P.M. Mon.–Thurs., 11 A.M.–midnight Fri.–Sat., 4–9 P.M. Sun., $20–26), in the Phoenix Grand Hotel, is a reliable place for fresh seafood and wood-fired pizzas. It's one of the fancier restaurants in town, but not stuffy.

One of the most popular fancy restaurants in town is **Alessandro's 120** (120 Commercial St. NE, 503/370-9951, 11:30 A.M.–2 P.M. Mon.–Fri., 5:30 P.M.–closing Sat., $12–26), with Salem's best Italian food served in a classy old downtown building filled with art.

Out of the main downtown, in the basement-dwelling **Morton's Bistro Northwest** (1128 Edgewater St. NW, 503/585-1113,

$17–27), you can find good food that leans toward the comforting rather than high culinary fashion. For example, a roasted chicken with mushrooms, capers, tomatoes, and greens is homey and tasty; a large selection of small plates (billed as the "theatre menu," $9–13) includes bacon-wrapped prawns, linguine with clams, and fish tacos. A good selection of reasonably priced wines is displayed on a wall of the restaurant.

U-pick farms are a delight from spring through fall in and around Salem. Cherries, strawberries, apples, peaches, plums, and blackberries are some of the bounty available. Early in June, the *Statesman Journal* puts out a list of local outlets in the area, describing what's available where and when, titled "Oregon Direct Market Association." Fruit stands are listed in this guide as well. Many concessionaires, such as **Bauman Farms** (12989 Howell Prairie Rd., 503/792-3524), offer both self-service harvest and over-the-counter sales. Several dozen agricultural products are available, including 10 berry varieties and pumpkins. Items such as fresh home-pressed apple cider and holiday gift packs round out the array. To get to Bauman's, take Route 99E one mile south of Woodburn to Howell Prairie Road. Following the signs, go about 0.5 miles to reach the stand.

INFORMATION

The **Travel Salem visitor information center** (181 High St. NE, 503/581-4325 or 800/874-7012, www.travelsalem.com, 8:30 A.M.–5 P.M. Mon.–Fri., 10 A.M.–5 P.M. Sat.) is located downtown.

The Salem *Statesman Journal* (503/399-6622) is sold throughout the Willamette Valley, central coast, and central Oregon. The newspaper's "Weekend" section features entertainment listings and reviews every Friday that cover the week to come. Although these listings focus on Salem, considerable attention is also given to events throughout the Willamette Valley, central Oregon, and the coast.

GETTING THERE AND AROUND

Salem's State and Center Streets run east–west; Commercial and Liberty Streets run north–south. East and West Nob Hill Streets run southeast. With a profusion of one-way streets and thoroughfares that end abruptly, it's important to keep your bearings. One helpful frame of reference is supplied by remembering that Commercial Street runs north–south along the Willamette River on the western edge of town.

Salem provides a lot of ways to get in and out of town. **Greyhound** (450 NE Church St., 503/362-2428) runs about five buses a day through Salem. **Amtrak** (13th St. and Oak St., 503/588-1551 or 800/872-7245) sits across from Willamette University and is close to Mission Mill Museum. The Salem **airport** (503/588-6314) is a few miles east of downtown. A Salem-to-Portland airport shuttle is run by **Hut Limousine Service** (503/364-4444, www.portlandairportshuttle.com, $35 one way).

Mass-transit bus service in town is run by **Salem Area Mass Transit (Cherriots)** (216 High St., 503/588-2877 or 503/588-2424, www.cherriots.org, $1.25). Terminals are in front of the courthouse.

SILVERTON

Silverton, located in the foothills of the Cascades about 10 miles east of Salem, is a thriving small town with a major attraction right out its back door. Don't rush past downtown Silverton; it's worth spending at least a few minutes wandering past or through the antique and decor shops. And don't be surprised to see a tall cross-dressing fellow out for coffee on a Saturday morning—that would be Mayor Stu, who knows firsthand that the Willamette Valley is still a place for pioneers.

Oregon Garden

The Oregon Garden (879 W. Main St., Silverton, 503/874-8100, www.oregongarden.org, 10 A.M.–6 P.M. daily May–Sept.,

© JUDY JEWELL

The Oregon Garden is home to a relatively modest but beautiful home designed by Frank Lloyd Wright.

10 A.M.–4 P.M. daily Oct.–Apr., $10 adults, $9 seniors, $8 students, half price off-season), while pleasant, has not yet become the world-class attraction originally envisioned. The botanical display was projected to grow to 250 acres—five times the size of the famous Butchart Gardens in Victoria, British Columbia—and was designed by a dream team of landscape architects with the backing of the state's dynamic nursery industry. Unfortunately, the garden was slow to develop, and the tourists were even slower to arrive. The financially beleaguered garden was purchased by Moonstone Hotel Properties in spring 2006, and a lovely new hotel and spa opened a couple of years later, making an overnight visit possible and attractive.

There are some lovely and innovative parts of the gardens. Especially intriguing is the wetlands section, which uses treated wastewater from Silverton to create a wetland. The water travels through a series of terraced ponds and wetland plants to a holding tank; from there it is used to irrigate the entire garden.

An attraction that makes the trip to the gardens worthwhile for architecture buffs is the **Gordon House** (879 W. Main St., Silverton, 503/874-6006, www.thegordonhouse.org, 11 A.M.–5 P.M. daily May–Oct., noon–4 P.M. daily Nov.–Apr., $5, reservations recommended for guided tour), a Frank Lloyd Wright–designed home located within the Oregon Garden complex. The house, originally located in Wilsonville, was moved to its current location in 2000, when the original property was sold and the new owners planned to demolish the house and rebuild to suit their own tastes. The modestly sized house is an example of Wright's populist Usonian style, and has beautiful western red cedar trim, many built-in drawers and cabinets, and lots of natural light. Terraces bring the outdoors in, and low ceilings in the bedrooms create a sense of retreat. Docents lead tours on the hour; this is the only way to see the upstairs of the house.

Accommodations and Food

The **Oregon Garden Resort** (895 W. Main St., 503/874-2500 or 800/966-6490, www.oregongardenresort.com, $109 and up) seems to be what the Oregon Garden needed. A main lodge provides space for weddings and other get-togethers; guest rooms are in a series of small six-unit buildings tucked behind the main lodge. All the guest rooms, which are decorated in a way that's pretty and upscale but not too designer-slick, have private patios or balconies and gas fireplaces; some are pet-friendly (as is part of the Oregon Garden itself). Many packages are offered, and special deals abound. Especially during the off season, this can be a surprisingly affordable getaway.

Should you decide to stay in town rather than at the gardens, a convenient and extensively remodeled option is the **Silverton Inn and Suites** (310 N. Water St., 503/873-1000, $75 and up), a once-lackluster motel that has been transformed into a stylish suite hotel with kitchenettes in most guest rooms. Silverton's other good option is the **Water Street Inn** (421 N. Water St., 503/873-3344, www.thewaterstreetinn.com, $125 and up), a renovated 1890s hotel that now operates as quite a lovely B&B.

Downtown Silverton's **Silver Grille** (206 E. Main St., 503/873-8000, 5–9 P.M. Wed.–Sat., $12–21) was, for a brief time, the *it* place to eat in the greater Salem area. Then the founding chef went to work for the Oregon Garden

Resort, and the place suffered. But Jerry is back, and the Silver Grille is once again a reliable place for a good dinner.

In a simple diner in downtown Silverton, you can find surprisingly good Thai food at **Thai Dish** (209A N. Water St., 503/873-8963, 11 A.M.–9 P.M. Mon.–Thurs., 11 A.M.–10 P.M. Fri., noon–10 P.M. Sat., noon–9 P.M. Sun., $8–13). Just down the block, **Mac's Place** (201 N. Water St., 503/873-2441) is a hoppin' blues joint.

The big annual "do" in Silverton is **Homer Davenport Days** (503/873-5211, www.davenportdays.com), usually held the first weekend in August, when locals enjoy crafts, food, music, and the spectacle of neighbors racing furniture down Main Street. Davenport was a nationally famous cartoonist in the 1930s and a Silverton favorite son. Most of the action takes place at Coolidge-McClain Park Friday evening and 10 A.M.–8 P.M. Saturday.

MOUNT ANGEL
◖ Mount Angel Abbey
Four miles northwest of Silverton off Route 214 and high above the rest of the Willamette

© JUDY JEWELL

Mount Angel Abbey is perched on a hill above the Willamette Valley.

Valley is Mount Angel Abbey. The abbey itself is perched above the faux-Bavarian town of Mount Angel; as you drive there you'll pass the neo-Gothic St. Mary's church, which is staffed by abbey monks.

The Benedictine abbey sits on a 300-foot hill overlooking cropland and Cascade vistas. From the bluff, look northward to Mount Hood, Mount St. Helens, Mount Adams, and, according to locals, on exceptionally clear days you can see Mount Rainier. The abbey **library,** designed by the famous Finnish architect Alvar Aalto, is an architectural highlight. The beautiful light and modern lines of the interior are nearly as inspiring as the texts on the shelves. But the texts are also pretty amazing, especially those housed in the Rare Book Room. Also worth checking out are the display cases in the lobby; the exhibits are invariably interesting.

The other Mount Angel Abbey building that's nearly mandatory to visit is the delightfully old-fashioned and noninterpretive museum (10–11:30 A.M. and 1–5 P.M. daily, free), which is tucked in a basement to the side of the main church (get a map from the librarian and ask to have the museum pointed out). Displays include religious artifacts such as a crown of thorns, crystals, and a huge collection of taxidermy, including an eight-legged calf.

The abbey's late-July Bach Festival features professional musicians in an idyllic setting; call for tickets months in advance (503/845-3321).

Guided tours of the abbey are offered by appointment. Meditative retreats can be arranged at the abbey's **retreat house** (503/845-3025, www.mountangelabbey.org, $77 includes all meals). Although the accommodations are ascetic, the peace of the surroundings and the beauty of the monks' rituals will deepen your personal reflections no matter what your spiritual orientation is.

Other Sights

The town of Mount Angel's other claim to fame is its **Oktoberfest** (541/845-9440), which takes place in mid-September, when thousands of folks flock here to enjoy the *Weingarten,* the beer garden, the oompah-pah of traditional German music, art displays, yodeling, and street dancing amid beautiful surroundings. The biggest attraction of all, however, is the food. Stuffed cabbage leaves, strudels, and an array of sausages are the stuff of legend in the Willamette Valley. In this vein, don't miss the Benedictine sisters' coffee cake and the Old World–style farmers market.

Bicyclists relish the foothills and farmland around Mount Angel, which are nearly devoid of traffic. Fall color is exceptional, and a varied topography ensures an eventful ride whatever the season. Lowland hop fields and filbert orchards give way to Christmas tree farms in the hills. On the way up, pumpkin and berry patches also break up the predominantly grassy terrain. This region is known as well for its crop of red fescue, a type of grass seed grown almost nowhere outside the northern Willamette Valley.

Another kind of ride is even more popular just up the road in Woodburn: The **Woodburn Dragstrip** (7730 Rte. 219, Woodburn, 503/982-4461, www.woodburndragstrip.com, $10 adults for most events) is an incredibly popular car-racing area.

For those who'd rather avoid the roar of the car engines, nurseries abound in the area as well. If you were to visit the **Wooden Shoe Bulb Company** (33814 S. Meridian Rd., Woodburn, 541/634-2243, www.woodenshoe.com, $10 per car weekends or $5 weekdays during the tulip festival) in late March and early April, it would colorfully illustrate Oregon's rites of spring. The 17-acre tulip farm is located near Woodburn; take Exit 271 off I-5 and follow Route 214 east. It will become Route 211 to Molalla; turn right at the flashing yellow light onto Meridian Road, and go 2 miles to the tulip fields. Afterward you can head south through the town of Monitor and reach Mount Angel via a delightful rural route.

Mount Angel's location an hour south of Portland makes it an excellent day trip. Just take Exit 272 for Woodburn off I-5 and follow the blue Silver Falls tour route signs. If you're approaching the Mount Angel Abbey from Salem off I-5, take the Chemawa Exit and follow the signs.

◖ SILVER FALLS STATE PARK

If this state park (22024 Silver Falls Hwy., Sublimity, 503/873-8681, ext. 31, www.oregonstateparks.org, $3 day use, $19–24 campsites, $39 cabins) were in California instead of the remote foothills east of the Willamette Valley, it would probably be designated a national park and be flooded with visitor facilities and people year-round. Instead, one of Oregon's largest and most spectacular state parks remains relatively quiet except during the summer. At that time, hordes seeking relief from the valley heat head up to this cool enclave of waterfalls 26 miles northeast of Salem. They come to see 10 major waterfalls 30–178 feet in height cascading off canyon walls in a forest filled with gargantuan Douglas fir, ferns, and bigleaf and vine maple. There are also yew, chinquapin, and hemlock trees. The best time to come is during fall foliage season when there are few visitors, just before icy roads and trail closures inhibit travel. Freezing east winds sometimes make the waterfalls appear like ice sculptures. In spring, the mid-April blooming of trilliums and yellow wood violets on the canyon bottom is another highlight.

Serious hikers will want to take on the seven-mile **Trail of Ten Falls**, which heads down into a fern-lined basalt gully going past all the waterfalls. The profusion of trees and moisture gives the air a special freshness, and when the sun hits some of the 10 waterfalls just right you can see rainbows. A two-car shuttle is recommended if you plan to hike the whole loop. The highlights of this 1930s-era Civilian Conservation Corps trail are 177-foot **South Falls** and 136-foot **North Falls.** The opportunity to walk behind these waterfalls attracts a lot of visitors, who follow the trail through a basalt overhang in the cleft of each cliff. Bikers and horseback riders also enjoy specially designated trails in this 8,300-acre paradise.

North Falls and South Falls are easily reached from the North Falls parking lot and the day-use area, respectively, so you don't have to hike the whole loop to see both. To get to the day-use area from the North Falls parking lot, drive several miles south up the hill (on Rte. 214), stopping after 1–2 miles to look back at a spectacular view of North Falls. Note that while leashed dogs are permitted on some trails at Silver Falls, they are not allowed on much of the Trail of Ten Falls.

A museum near the day-use parking area features vintage photos from the area's incarnation as a logging site founded by land speculator James "Silver" Smith (so named for his penchant for carrying around a sack of silver dollars), and wildlife exhibits provide a nice introduction. A short distance from the museum is a viewpoint and the trailhead to South Falls. Like the North Falls trail, this is a steep ascent of about 0.25 miles.

The park's campground has 46 tent sites, 52 sites for trailers or motor homes up to 35 feet long, and 10 log cabins. Large groups (up to 75 people) can rent dormitory-style bunkhouses, called "ranches," for $100 per night. Tent sites are open May–October; the RV campground and one of the "ranches" are open year-round. In addition to hiking, swimming, and biking, there are stables near the park's entrance and a horse camp.

If you plan to visit the park from Portland, leave I-5 at Woodburn and follow rural Route 214 south through Mount Angel and Silverton. From Salem, either drive east on Route 213 to Silverton or approach the park farther south by taking Route 22 east out of Salem and following the signs northeast to the park from Sublimity. Although it's longer, the latter route enables you to do a loop from Salem to Silver Creek Falls on different roads, taking in more varied landscapes in the process.

The main drag in Silverton, Water Street (a.k.a. Route 214, the Silver Creek Falls Highway), heads south out of town toward the park. En route, stop at the chamber of commerce outdoor information kiosk (421 S. Water St., 503/873-5615) to pick up a Silverton directory map and a park folder. Traveling south and eventually east en route to the park on

Route 214, the road climbs up into gently undulating hills past Christmas tree farms and nursery stock. A dearth of signs and a distance that seems longer than the posted 15 miles from town will have you second-guessing these directions until you come to the North Falls parking lot. While North Falls is a few miles north of the visitor services and facilities of Silver Creek Falls State Park headquarters at the day-use area, you can park your car at the trailhead here and skip the admission kiosk and shopping-mall-sized parking lot down the road.

OPAL CREEK

The old-growth forests and emerald pools of Opal Creek were an environmental battleground for years until a land swap with a timber company who owned the logging rights. Opal Creek's 31,000-acre watershed, which includes a grove of 1,000-year-old 250-foot red cedar, has been called the most intact old-growth ecosystem on the West Coast.

To get here from Salem, take Route 22 for 19 miles east to Mehama. At the second flashing yellow light (at the corner with Swiss Village), turn left off Route 22 onto Little North Fork Santiam River Road past the State Forestry office and go about 15 miles toward the Elkhorn Recreation Area. Stay on this route until Forest Service Road 2209 (mostly gravel) and be sure to veer left, uphill, at the Y intersection. About 6 miles past the Willamette National Forest sign, a locked gate will bar your car from proceeding farther down Road 2209. Park and follow the trail to a large wooden map displaying various hiking options.

While old-growth trees abound not far from the parking lot, be sure to cross over to the south side of the North Fork of the Little Santiam River (indicated by trailside signs). Here you can take in the placid Opal Pool, a small circular translucent aquamarine catch-basin at the base of a cascade that cuts through limestone. Located several miles from the parking lot over gently rolling terrain, Opal Pool is the perfect day-hike destination.

There aren't just trees and pools of water at Opal Creek; the **Opal Creek Ancient Forest Center** (503/892-2782, http://opalcreek.org) is an environmental education center with a few cabins for rent ($125 and up). A nearby Bureau of Land Management campground, **Elkhorn Valley**, is a good place to camp and stage a day trip to Opal Creek.

DETROIT LAKE

It's a Salem tradition to take to the hills via Route 22 along the North Santiam River to enjoy the fishing and camping at Detroit Lake. This large and busy 400-foot-deep reservoir is known for its boating, waterskiing, swimming, and fishing for rainbow trout, landlocked Chinook, and kokanee. Boat rentals are available at the marina. Because the reservoir was built for water storage, during drought years it can be drawn down enough to make recreation unappealing.

Although most Detroit Lake campers stay at the **Detroit Lake State Recreation Area** (503/854-3346, reservations 800/452-5687, www.oregonstateparks.org, $19–24) on the lake's north shore, the more remote south-shore **Cove Creek** (Blowout Rd., 503/854-3366, www.fs.fed.us/r6/Willamette, $18) is much more peaceful. With 63 sites, flush toilets, pay showers, a boat launch, and other amenities, it's still not exactly a wilderness experience, but it's quite pleasant. Campsites are located in a lush second-growth Douglas fir forest against a slope. Because there are no individual RV hookups, dump sites, or phones, Cove Creek is designed more for car campers than for people looking for a place to park a rig long-term. The campground is located east of Detroit off Blowout Road. Not accepting reservations, a sign on the highway will announce if the site has reached capacity.

BREITENBUSH
◖ Breitenbush Hot Springs

Breitenbush Hot Springs Retreat and Conference Center (503/854-3320, www.breitenbush.com) offers natural hot springs, trails forested with old growth, as well as a wide variety of programs aimed at healing body, mind, and spirit. Set in the Cascade foothills, this onetime Native American encampment's artesian-flow hot springs have attracted people for healing throughout the ages. The hot springs pools, set variously in forest and meadow, contain 30 freely occurring minerals, including lithium. Music, storytelling, yoga, and superb vegetarian cuisine are also part of the Breitenbush experience. Although many visitors come to Breitenbush to take part in an organized workshop (such as yoga, meditation, or spirituality), it's also possible to come on your own for a personal retreat. Know before you go that most hot-springs bathers forgo the option of clothing.

The retreat cabins are Spartan but sufficient. All have electricity and heat, and some have indoor plumbing. Rates are $97 (weekend rates; weekdays are a few dollars cheaper) per person for a cabin without a bathroom (there are a couple of bathhouses) or about $115 for a cabin with a bath (bring your own bedding or pay $16 extra), including three sumptuous vegetarian meals and use of the facilities and waters. Single visitors may sometimes be assigned a cabin-mate unless they specify otherwise (and pay extra). Large tents on platforms are also available June–October for $72 per person, or you can camp in your own tent for $61. Day-use fees for hot springs and other facilities are $13–26; call ahead to make sure there's room for a day-use visitor. Individual all-you-can-eat lunches or dinners for daytime visitors cost $11. Be sure to bring your own caffeine if that's something that you require. Do not bring alcoholic beverages.

Near Breitenbush are such remarkable natural areas as Breitenbush Gorge, Opal Creek, Bull of the Woods, and Jefferson Park; for more information contact the Detroit Ranger Station at 503/854-3366.

On-site you'll find the Spotted Owl Trail near the entrance of the Breitenbush parking lot. In addition to this and other trails (get maps at the reception desk), sacred sweat-lodge ceremonies conducted by Native Americans are offered once a month.

To get to Breitenbush from Salem, take Route 22 to the town of Detroit. Turn at the gas station—the only one in town—onto Forest Service Road 46. Drive 10 miles to Cleator Bend Campground. Go 100 feet past the campground and take a right over the bridge across Breitenbush River. Follow the signs, taking every left turn after the bridge, to the Breitenbush parking lot.

If Breitenbush is full, **All Seasons Motel** (130 Breitenbush Rd., 503/854-3421 or 877/505-8879, www.allseasonsmotel.net, $49 and up), at Route 22 and Forest Service Road 46, is clean and comfy. The ecumenical spirit is on display in the rooms with Eastern holy books alongside Gideon Bibles. It's not at all inconvenient to drive 15 minutes from here to the retreat center.

Cleator Bend

On the way up Route 22 to Breitenbush Hot Springs, Cleator Bend (Rte. 22, Detroit, 503/854-3366, www.fs.fed.us/r6/Willamette, May–Sept., $12) offers a campground close enough to the Breitenbush Hot Springs Retreat Center and facilities to permit day use there. Nearby, the Breitenbush River has good fishing. There are nine sites for trailers or motor homes up to 16 feet long, as well as picnic tables and fire grills. On Forest Service Road 46, you'll pass several other campgrounds between Route 22 and Breitenbush.

OLALLIE LAKE

To the east of Breitenbush, and almost directly north of Mount Jefferson, Olallie Lake is one of the nicest camping and hiking getaways in the area, with superb views of Mount Jefferson from the lake. The lake has a small cabin resort (www.olallielakeresort.com), which was closed and undergoing some badly needed cabin rebuilding in 2009 with plans to reopen in summer 2010; see the website for rates. The resort also manages the Paul Dennis campground adjacent to the cabin area ($14 campsite, $50 yurt) and rents rowboats and canoes. Olallie Lake is along the Pacific Crest Trail, and there are hiking trails galore, many leading to other small lakes. In the early summer, wildflowers are an attraction; late in summer, this is a great place to pick wild huckleberries. The season up here is pretty short—snows usually keep the resort closed until July.

From the Detroit area, head north and east on Forest Service Road 46, then turn right on Forest Service Road 4220 (a rough gravel road) and follow it 13 miles to the lake.

MOUNT JEFFERSON

Prepare your muscles for a soak in the pools at Breitenbush by hiking on Mount Jefferson, Oregon's second-highest peak, 10,495 feet above sea level. This snowcapped symmetrical volcanic cone dominates the Oregon Cascades horizon between Mount Hood to the north and the Three Sisters to the south. Unlike Mount Hood, Mount Jefferson is rarely visible to motorists approaching from the west.

Twelve miles east of Detroit on Route 22, turn left; follow Forest Service Road 2243 (Whitewater Creek Rd.) 7.5 miles to the Whitewater Creek trailhead. Then it's an easy 4.5-mile hike to Jefferson Park. This is the northern base of the mountain and features a plethora of lakes and wildflowers. The alpine meadows are full of purple and yellow lupine and red Indian paintbrush in July. On the way up, wild strawberries and red huckleberries can provide a delectable snack. For a special experience during the summer, start the walk after 5 P.M. when there's a full moon and the trail is bathed in soft lunar light.

Above Jefferson Park, the ascent of the dormant volcano's cone is a precarious endeavor and should only be attempted by truly experienced climbers. You'll reach the bottom of Whitewater Glacier at 7,000 feet. Thereafter, climbing routes steepen to 45 degrees and snow and rock ridges crumble when touched. Near the top, the rocks aren't solid enough to allow the use of ropes or other forms of climbing protection; going down is even more dangerous than going up. Even if you head up the more sedate south face, you can expect difficulties due to the instability of the final 400 feet of rock on the pinnacle. It must be emphasized that climbers regularly die on Jefferson.

© MIKE RUMSEY PHOTOGRAPHY

Mount Jefferson from the Pacific Crest Trail

Those who elect not to make the ascent may also run into problems. Sometimes the mosquitoes in Jefferson Park are bloodthirsty enough to pierce thick clothing. On occasion the area is so crowded with day-use visitors and folks trekking the nearby Pacific Crest Trail that this place seems more like a city park than a mountain wilderness. No matter; the sight of Mount Jefferson in alpenglow at sunset or shrouded in moonlight will make you forget the intrusions of humankind or the elements.

Corvallis

The name "Corvallis" refers to the city's pastoral setting in the "Heart of the Valley." But just as much as its physical setting, it's the culture of Oregon State University that defines Corvallis. Everything from the coffeehouses and used bookstores to the pizza joints and network of biking trails seems to owe its existence to the ivy-covered walls of academe. It has been this way for a long time; Cascadia, the quintessential college town in the novel *A New Life* by the late Oregon State University professor Bernard Malamud, was modeled on Corvallis.

Although Corvallis isn't a huge travel destination, its beauty, tranquility, and central location in the heart of the valley recommend it as a base from which to explore the bird sanctuaries, the Coast Range, and nearby historic communities. In town, you'll be struck by the abundance of stately old trees, some dating back to the first pioneers, who arrived in 1847. Streets with wide bike lanes and scenic routes for cyclists that parallel the Willamette and Mary's Rivers also contribute to the idyllic time-warp feeling. This is especially the case in summer, when many students leave town.

In springtime, the daffodil-lined approach to Corvallis on Route 99W is made even more glorious by the Coast Range and its highest mountain, 4,097-foot **Mary's Peak,** to the west over the hay meadows. During much of the winter, rain and fog obscure the summit from view.

SIGHTS
Downtown
Although a good chunk of the town's real estate is taken up by the OSU campus, Corvallis has a thriving downtown with a splendid path along the Willamette River. A number of restaurants face onto the riverfront.

The **Benton County Courthouse** (120 NW 4th St., 541/766-6756), near 4th and 5th Streets and Monroe Avenue, dates from 1888 and is the oldest functioning courthouse in the lower Willamette Valley. You can't miss its large white clock tower, but go inside to get the old-fashioned feel of the place. (Be sure to check out the basement bathrooms.)

Also downtown is the **Corvallis Art Center** (7th St. and Madison Ave., 541/754-1551, noon–5 P.M. Tues.–Sun.), located in the renovated 1889 Episcopal church near Central Park. It sells local crafts and hosts weekly lunchtime concerts.

A large concentration of historic homes can be found in Corvallis, including many in neighborhoods close to downtown. Download walking-tour maps of various neighborhoods from www.visitcorvallis.com; one interesting tour visits ranch houses from the 1950s.

Campus
The parklike 500-acre campus of **Oregon State University** (OSU), home to 15,200 students (follow the signs to Jefferson Ave. or Monroe Ave., 541/737-0123, www.oregonstate.edu), an 1868 land-grant institution, is the major hub of activity in town, with a slew of eateries, bookstores, and craft boutiques on its periphery. Cultural activities on campus include lectures, concerts, theater productions, films, and art exhibits. Many are free and open to the public.

belly dancer at the Corvallis Farmers Market

Visit Corvallis from the end of February through mid-March and you can watch ewes giving birth in the lambing barns at the university's **Sheep Center** (7565 NW Oak Creek Dr., 541/737-4854, 9 A.M.–3 P.M. daily). To get to the center from downtown Corvallis, head west on Harrison Boulevard to the 53rd Street intersection. Continue west through the intersection on NW Oak Creek Drive (a.k.a. Walnut St.). A sign after 1.8 miles will indicate the road to the center; this one-lane road has turnouts allowing you to yield to oncoming traffic.

While the notion of one of these fleecy specimens on a dinner plate might seem akin to eating Bambi, this facility's research has helped establish Oregon lamb as a gourmet product. Thanks to a diet of nutritious grasses indigenous to Northwest soils, Oregon lambs are larger and richer in flavor than their better-publicized New Zealand counterparts. The barns are open every day during daylight hours. While there are no formal guides, student staffers and informational fliers will help answer questions. The sight of a newborn standing and walking a few minutes after birth is amazing to first-time visitors.

The university also maintains 11,500 acres of woodlands, notably **McDonald Experimental Forest** and **Peavy Arboretum,** accessible 8 miles north of Corvallis on Route 99W, which feature hiking trails as well as the chance to see the rare Fender's blue butterfly. The species had been thought extinct for 50 years until a habitat was discovered here in 1990. This ecosystem serves primarily as a living laboratory for the university's Forestry Department.

Benton County Historical Society
Six miles west of Corvallis on Route 34 is the town of **Philomath,** home to the **Benton County Historical Society** (1101 Main St., Philomath, 541/929-6230, 10 A.M.–4:30 P.M. Tues.–Sat., free). Looms, carriages, printing presses, and other pioneer-history exhibits are mildly diverting, but the real star is the 1867 Georgian-style brick structure housing the collection. Just look for the imposing building on the right side of the highway as you head toward the coast.

Tyee Winery
Located 10 miles off Route 99W south of Corvallis on the way up into the Coast Range

is Tyee Wine Cellars (26335 Greenberry Rd., Corvallis, 541/753-8754, noon–5 P.M. Sat.–Sun. Apr.–Dec., noon–5 P.M. Fri.–Mon. mid-June–Labor Day). It's easy to incorporate a stop here into trips to nearby destinations such as Finley Wildlife Refuge, Mary's Peak, or Alsea Falls. Pinot gris, pinot noir, chardonnay, and Gewürztraminer are featured. After wine-tasting, you can enjoy a picnic on the grounds of this historic farm site or walk a 1.5-mile loop to beaver ponds. Several other wineries are also located in the area; see www.bentoncountywineries.com if you want to explore some of the smaller operations.

Natural Attractions

The pastures of Lebanon and Brownsville east of Corvallis are good places to spot bald eagles. Venture out to the fields (beginning in February) when sheep are lambing to see eagles soaring above the newborn lambs. In the winter, grass seed farms outside Albany, Coburg, and Junction City attract tundra swans.

West of Corvallis, two spots have drawn seekers of natural beauty and solitude for many years. Mary's Peak and Alsea Falls are each a short drive from Route 34, a scenic route to Waldport, which branches off U.S. 20 southwest of Philomath.

Mary's Peak (541/563-3211, www.fs.fed.us/r6/siuslaw) sits about 12 miles southwest of Corvallis. From I-5, take U.S. 20 into Corvallis, then Route 34 to Philomath. From here it's 9 miles west to the road's Coast Range Summit (1,230 feet). A sign north of the highway points the way to a 10-mile drive to the top of the Coast Range's highest peak (4,097 feet) on Forest Service Road 30, the only road on the peak's south side. Along the way, pretty cascades, interesting rock outcroppings, and over-the-shoulder views of the Cascades on the eastern horizon intensify the anticipation of this mountaintop Kalapuyan vision-quest site.

When you get to the parking lot at the end of the road, the view is impressive—but don't stop there. If it's a clear day, take the short walk across the meadows to either of the two summit lookouts for perspectives on Mounts Hood and Jefferson, the Three Sisters to the east (reportedly eight Cascades peaks in total are potentially visible from here), and the Pacific Ocean at the base of the Coast Range to the west.

The summit, thanks to its status as a federally designated botanical area, remains untouched by clear-cuts that speckle the forests nearby. A biome unique to the Coast Range exists up here, with such flora as alpine phlox, beargrass, iris, tiger lily, Indian paintbrush, purple lupine, and the blue-green noble fir. Exceptionally large species of this fragrant tree grow on the Meadows Edge Trail. This trail connects to a primitive car-camping area with 16 sites (Mar. 21–Oct. 31, $4 per night) 2 miles below the summit. It's part of a 9-mile network of trails around the upper slopes of the mountain.

You'll also find hemlock, fir, and grand fir. Local creeks are home to the unique Mary's Peak salamander, and the surrounding woods host bald eagles, red-tailed hawks, spotted owls, and Clark's nutcrackers—seldom seen west of the Cascades. There are also, very occasionally, black bears. When it's clear, Mary's Peak is a prime viewing spot in western Oregon for the Perseid meteor shower in August.

Snow, an infrequent visitor to most Coast Range slopes, can often be found here in winter, even at lower elevations. In fact, the road is sometimes impassable without chains from late fall until early spring. A Sno-Park permit is required for day use November 15–April 15. Contact the Waldport Ranger Station (541/563-3211) for more information.

Farther down Route 34 is the town of **Alsea.** The adjoining Lobster Valley area drew many countercultural refugees in the 1970s, a portion of whom have remained to become farmers and craftspeople. The greenness of the valley surrounded by Coast Range foothills recalled the lower alpine regions of Europe enough to inspire the nickname "Little Scotland."

South of here, a paved-over logging road through the tall timbers of the Coast Range can take you back to the Willamette Valley on a remote scenic byway. Look for a sign that says "Alsea Falls, South Fork Road/Monroe." There's also a campground (www.blm.gov/or) with 16 sites, piped water, pit toilets, picnic tables, and fire rings for $10 per night. You'll follow the Alsea River much of the way until you come to the sloping parking lot near Alsea Falls on the east side of the road. A short trail leads you to a picturesque cascade, ideal for a picnic. The road continues through once-active logging towns into farming country and the Finley Wildlife Refuge south of Corvallis.

From here, Route 99W goes north to Corvallis or south to Junction City and Eugene.

SPORTS AND RECREATION

The OSU **Beavers** (www.osubeavers.com for schedules and tickets) dominate the sports scene in Corvallis. In fact, unless you're a fan, you might want to avoid town if the Beavs are playing the University of Oregon Ducks. During the 2008 presidential election, the OSU basketball team had a little extra atten-

WILLAMETTE BIRD SANCTUARIES

The federal government established several bird sanctuaries between Salem and Eugene in the mid-1960s because of the encroachment of urbanization and agriculture on the winter habitat of the dusky Canada goose. This species now comes to **Baskett Slough National Wildlife Refuge** (NWR) west of Salem, **Ankeny NWR** southwest of Salem, and **Finley NWR** south of Corvallis each October after summering in Alaska's Copper River Delta. Refuge ecosystems mesh forest, cropland, and riparian environments to attract hummingbirds, swans, geese, sandhill cranes, ducks, egrets, herons, plovers, sandpipers, hawks and other raptors, wrens, woodpeckers, and dozens of other avian ambassadors. Migrating waterfowl begin showing up in the Willamette Valley in mid-October. By mid-March, large numbers of Canada geese, tundra swans, and a variety of ducks descend on the refuge.

The pamphlet "Birds of Willamette Valley Refuges" (available from Refuge Manager, Western Oregon Refuges, 26208 Finley Refuge Rd., Corvallis 97337, 541/757-7236, www.fws.gov/willamettevalley/finley/) details the best months to bird-watch, the frequency of sightings, and the locations of hundreds of kinds of birds.

To maintain the sanctity of the birds' habitat, the refuges restrict birders by closing some trails in winter; other trails farther from feeding grounds are kept open year-round. A hike that can be enjoyed any time of year is Finley NWR's one-mile **Woodpecker Loop.** A variety of plant communities exists due to the Kalapuyan Native American people's field-burning followed by pioneer logging and cattle-grazing. Its location on the border between the Coast Range and the Willamette Valley also contributes to the diversity. Forests of oak and Douglas fir as well as a mixed-deciduous grove combine with marshes to provide a wide range of habitats. Look for the rare pileated woodpecker in the deciduous forest. The loop's trailhead is reached by taking Route 99W (from Corvallis) to Refuge Road. Look for the footpath on the right after driving three miles. A drop box has a pamphlet with pictures and information on the birds, wildlife, and plant communities.

Ankeny NWR is located 12 miles south of Salem off I-5 at Exit 243, and Baskett Slough NWR lies northwest of Rickreall on Route 22. Visit fall through spring for the best chance to see ducks, geese, swans, and raptors.

In recent years the proliferation of Canada geese in the lower Willamette Valley has compelled people to question if the refuges have been too successful. Farmers complain that the birds interfere with crops. State wildlife managers are currently rethinking the protections accorded to the migratory fowl. After seeing the dwindling numbers of the state bird, the western meadowlark, in the Willamette Valley due to human encroachment, let's hope the powers that be can reach a healthy balance.

tion—they are coached by President Barack Obama's brother-in-law, Craig Robinson.

The **Osborn Aquatic Center** (1940 NW Highland Dr., 541/766-7946, $4 adults, $3.50 youth 7–17, $2.75 children 6 and under) has both indoor and outdoor pools, including a large outdoor recreational pool with lots of play equipment.

ENTERTAINMENT AND EVENTS

Block 15 (300 SW Jefferson Ave., 541/758-2077), a brewpub, brings in a good mix of music—jazz, blues, bluegrass—on a pretty regular, though not nightly, basis. It's a pleasant low-key place to hang out, with a strong emphasis on doing business sustainably. A good spot for cocktails and occasional music is **CrowBar** (214 SW 2nd St., 541/753-7373), tucked behind the American Dream pizza in a secluded alley spot.

Other live-music standbys and typical college taverns include the **Peacock Tavern** (125 SW 2nd St., 541/754-8522) and **Squirrel's Tavern** (100 SW 2nd St., 541/753-8057), which brings in music most Saturday nights during the school year.

The Corvallis drama scene coalesces around the **Majestic Theater** (115 SW 2nd St., 541/766-6976), a restored 1913 vaudeville house. Close by is the excellent **Grassroots Books and Music** (227 SW 2nd St., 541/754-7558).

Aside from OSU Beavers football games, the biggest event in Corvallis is **Da Vinci Days** (541/757-6363, www.davinci-days.org), held the third weekend in July to carry on the creative spirit embodied by the genius for whom the festival is named. Sculpt, play chess on a computer, take part in a drama, or just sit and listen to music as Corvallis's vibrant artistic and scientific community shares its inspirational bounty. New vaudeville acts and food booths also showcase the region's creativity. Kinetic sculpture races—these must be seen to be believed—along with lectures by scientists and interactive exhibits impart an intellectual air to the proceedings. The festival takes place on the Oregon State University campus and in Central Park, between 9th and 11th Streets. One-day admission is $10 for adults, $5 for kids; full weekend tickets are $15 adults, $10 kids. Because festival events are spread out all over town, a car or a bike is necessary to take full advantage of it all.

Another big Corvallis celebration is the **Corvallis Fall Festival** (541/752-9655, www.corvallisfallfestival.com). This gathering of artists and craftspeople is now in its second decade. Nonstop varied entertainment and a block of food concessions, including an Oregon wine garden, provide a backdrop for this hotbed of creative ferment the fourth weekend in September in Central Park, between 6th and 8th Streets and Monroe and Madison Avenues.

Two area musical events held each summer are the **Memorial Day Bluegrass Festival** at Airlie Winery about 20 miles northwest of Corvallis (15305 Dunn Forest Rd., Monmouth, 503/838-6013, www.airliewinery.com) and Sweet Home's **Oregon Jamboree** (541/367-8800, www.oregonjamboree.com), Oregon's largest country music event. In years past, Merle Haggard, Wynonna Judd, Dwight Yoakam, LeAnn Rimes, and other big names have appeared for this early August event, organized to help timber-dependent communities cope economically with the era of limits in Oregon forests.

ACCOMMODATIONS

A prime place to stay along the river on the edge of downtown Corvallis is the **C Holiday Inn Express** (781 NE 2nd St., 541/752-0800 or 888/465-4329, www.hiexpress.com, $105 and up). It's within an easy and pleasant walk of the downtown riverfront restaurants; get a river-view guest room and perhaps you'll see an eagle flying upriver early in the morning.

Also along the river near downtown is the **Super 8 Motel** (407 NW 2nd St., 541/758-8088, $70 and up). It's nothing fancy, but the location is good.

With a sister location in Reedsport, **Salbasgeon Suites** (1730 NW 9th St.,

541/753-4320 or 800/965-8808, www.salbasgeon.com, $120 and up) is situated in the heart of Corvallis's business district, just a jaunt from dining and shops. Guests have access to the large indoor heated swimming pool, the sauna, and a gym as well as in-room high-speed Internet access. There's also a good restaurant on-site.

The **Hilton Garden Inn** (2500 SW Western Blvd., 541/752-5000 or 800/445-8667, $107 and up) is practically part of the OSU campus; it's located near Reser Stadium (the football stadium), Gill Coliseum (the basketball arena), and the OSU Conference Center. It's a very comfortable hotel with good amenities for business travelers.

The **Hanson Country Inn** (795 SW Hanson St., 541/752-2919, www.hcinn.com, $95 and up) gives you the feeling you're way out of town even though it's actually within walking distance of campus. Antiques, canopy beds, 1920s woodwork, and a book-lined library warm up the interior. On the outside, a hillside overlooking the Hanson farm offers a feeling of tranquility. A two-bedroom cottage, ideal for families, sits behind the main house.

If you really do want to get out into the countryside, consider a farm stay at the **Leaping Lamb** (20368 Honey Grove Rd., Alsea, 541/487-4966 or 877/820-6132, www.leapinglambfarm.com, $125 and up), where a private two-bedroom cabin with cooking facilities (basic breakfast items supplied) is perfect for families. It's well situated for hikes into the nearby forest or for just communing with farm animals.

Camping

Camping in this part of the Willamette Valley can be delightful, especially in late spring and early autumn.

About 14 miles east of Sweet Home off U.S. 20 is **Cascadia State Park,** (reservations 800/452-5687, Mar.–late Oct., $14 plus $6 reservation fee), near the banks of the South Santiam River. Rocks form great swimming holes. A nearby waterfall, a cave with petroglyphs, an old-growth Douglas fir, and a hand pump to draw up mineral water are other appeals. Also along U.S. 20 are superlative boating and fishing on Green Peter and Foster Lake reservoirs. Such amenities as piped water, flush toilets, and firewood are available, and a store is located less than 1 mile away.

The campground at **Mary's Peak** (541/750-7000, $10) is open mid-May–mid-September; the final stretch of road to this spot is unsuitable for trailers. It's about 19 miles from town.

RV campers can stay at **Benton Oaks** (110 SW 53rd St., 541/766-6259, $25 and up) year-round; tent campers are welcome in the summer. Rates are jacked up during football weekends. This is a pleasant county campground located in a grove of increasingly rare Oregon white oaks at the county fairgrounds.

FOOD

The riverfront stretch of downtown is home to several good restaurants. **◖ Big River Restaurant and Bar** (101 N. Jackson St., 541/757-0694, 11 A.M.–2 P.M. and 5–9:30 P.M. Mon.–Thurs., 11 A.M.–2 P.M. and 5–11:30 P.M. Fri.–Sat., $15–28) is a lively hip restaurant with good food, much of it from local producers. Seafood is a good bet.

Also along the river is **Aqua Seafood Restaurant** (151 NW Monroe Ave., 541/752-0262, 4:30–closing Tues.–Sat., $20–30), which features Pacific Rim Hawaiian cuisine, including coriander salmon "popsicles." The Hawaiian chef comes from Roy's, one of that state's top restaurants.

In the heart of downtown, **Aomatsu's Grill** (122 NW 3rd St., 541/752-1410, 11:30 A.M.–2 P.M. and 5–10 P.M. Mon.–Fri., 5–10 P.M. Sat., lunch $8–9, dinner $10–22) is an unpretentious restaurant with good sushi as well as teriyaki and bento.

Near the university, **Bombs Away Cafe** (2527 Monroe St., 541/757-7221, 11 A.M.–10 P.M. Mon.–Fri., 5–10 P.M. Sat., $7–17) is an always-filled-to-capacity 65-seat restaurant with colorful murals on the walls, frequent live music, and lines of waiting-list hopefuls anxious to sample finger food made with the freshest ingredients and organic produce.

Perhaps the best place to provision a picnic is the deli at **First Alternative Co-op** (1007 SE 3rd St., 541/753-3115), which you'll encounter as you come into town via Route 99W from the south.

Another spot that's wholesome and hippie-ish is **Nearly Normal's** (109 NW 15th St., 541/753-0791, 8 A.M.–9 P.M. Mon.–Fri., 9 A.M.–9 P.M. Sat., $6–10), whose jungle of greenery and mismatched artsy-kitschy decor does justice to its name (inspired by a character in a Tom Robbins novel). The vegetarian "gonzo cuisine" (no meat here) is tasty—try the tempeh enchiladas or cheesy spinach lasagna— and the ambiance is relaxed and friendly.

It doesn't get much fresher or more local than lunch at **Gathering Together Farm** (25159 Grange Hall Rd., 541/929-4270, 11 A.M.–2 P.M. Tues.–Wed., 11 A.M.–2 P.M. and 6–9 P.M. Thurs.–Fri., 9 A.M.–2 P.M. Sat., lunch about $10). Lunches are the mainstay of this farm kitchen; during the winter, when produce is harder to come by, it might include a house-made sausage with sauerkraut, potatoes, and carrots. Three-course dinners cost $23 and can start with a beet and salted-honey soup followed by a duck breast with blackberry sauce, carrot puree, and chard with chocolate cake to finish.

Corvallis also has a farmers market that takes place 9 A.M.–1 P.M. Saturday late May– late October in the City Hall parking lot (6th St. and Monroe Ave.). There is also a market held 8 A.M.–1 P.M. Wednesday at the Benton County Fairgrounds (110 SW 53rd St.). Look for excellent Alsea Acre Alpine's goat cheese and the Co-op's calzones along with other regional staples.

INFORMATION

The **Corvallis Visitor's Information Center** (553 NW Harrison Blvd., 541/757-1544 or 800/334-8118, www.visitcorvallis.com) maintains a good website.

To catch up on local events, read the *Corvallis Gazette Times* (www.gtconnect.com).

KOAC (550 AM) is an excellent public radio station with a top-notch news team and classical music offerings. Serving much of western Oregon, KOAC can be picked up in remote coastal and mountain communities.

GETTING THERE AND AROUND

Greyhound and **Valley Retriever** (153 NW 4th St., 541/757-1797) operate every day, with routes north and south as well as west to the coastal town of Newport.

Corvallis Transit (501 Madison Ave., 541/757-6988, Mon.–Sat., $0.75) operates city buses.

Corvallis is laid out logically, and it's easy to get anywhere within 15 minutes. With 47 miles of bike trails and 13 miles of paved bike paths, it's not surprising the city has garnered kudos from national media for its commuter-friendly traffic arteries. Recreational bikers sing the praises of the Corvallis-to-Philomath bike path. It begins along the Willamette River in downtown Corvallis and continues 8 miles through rural Benton County before ending in Philomath.

ALBANY

Twelve miles east of Corvallis on U.S. 20 is Albany, and though you wouldn't know it as you drive the long commercial strip between I-5 and downtown, it has more historic homes than any other city in Oregon. More than 350 Victorian houses bespeak Albany's golden age, from 1849 to the early 20th century, when wheat was the primary crop and steamships and railroads exported Willamette Valley produce and flour. Twenty-eight trains departed this commercial hub daily in 1910. The **Albany Visitors Association** (250 Broadalbin St. SW, Suite 110, 541/928-0911 or 800/526-2256, www.albanyvisitors.com) and an information gazebo at the corner of 8th Avenue and Ellsworth Street have maps and pamphlets (downloadable from the website) about the three historic districts that cover 100 blocks. While you're here, be sure to get directions to the **Monteith House** (518 W. 2nd

Ave., 800/526-2256), the oldest pioneer frame building in Albany, dating to 1849. Inquire about the **Albany Regional Museum,** whose exhibits on the Kalapuya Native American people and Albany's pioneer and Victorian eras provide a good introduction.

In their heyday, two Albany residential districts were rivals. The **Hackleman District,** Ellsworth to Madison Streets and 2nd to 8th Avenues, was a working-class neighborhood that at one time featured a furniture factory and a railroad station. These houses are practical but rich in Victorian nuance. The adjoining **Monteith District,** Elm to Ellsworth Streets and 2nd to 12th Avenues, was home to wealthy merchants and businessmen; the houses here are grand and opulent.

Also imbued with Willamette Valley history are the area's charming **covered bridges.** These canopied crossings protected the wooden trusses from rain, extending the life of the bridges by several decades. By the late 1930s, many of the 300 or so covered bridges in the state had fallen into disrepair or were replaced by modern steel and concrete spans. Statewide, 48 remain, with 30 in the Willamette Valley. A pamphlet available from the Albany Visitors Association lays out a self-guided tour of eight bridges within 20–30 minutes' drive from the Albany-Corvallis area. All of these fall within an 8-mile radius of Scio, a town 13 miles northeast of Albany on Route 226.

To get to Scio, head north on I-5 for 10 or 15 minutes, then take Exit 233 and follow the signs east to Route 226. Of all the bridges in this loop, don't miss the bright-red paint job of the Shimanek Bridge and the creek-side splendor of the Larwood Bridge. In Scio itself a small **Scio Historical Depot Museum** (39004 NE 1st Ave., Scio, 503/394-2199, 1–4 P.M. Sat.–Sun.) survives on donations. The hodgepodge of Oregon Trail memorabilia, wood carvings, 19th-century newspapers, and family heirlooms in this oddly curated assemblage can be more affecting than the slicker high-tech displays you'll encounter elsewhere in the state.

Prime time for a stroll down Albany's memory lane is during the Christmas holiday season. In December (usually the second Sunday), annual old-fashioned **parlor tours** (800/526-5526, $10 adults, $8 seniors, free for children 12 and under) let you revel in eggnog, snapping fires, and frontier hospitality as a guest at a number of Victorian homes. Visitors are welcomed by hostesses at each home and are permitted to walk through the parlor and other open rooms. Entertainment and homemade refreshments are part of the festivities. Historical district hay-wagon and trolley caroling tours are part of the package and can get you in the holiday spirit.

Interior tours of historic houses are available during the last weekend in July ($10 adults, $8 seniors). Visitors are invited to walk through the gardens and entire interiors of several homes; background anecdotes are supplied by guides. Old-fashioned quilts and dolls complement the tour, as do many people in turn-of-the-20th-century dress strolling the avenues. At all times of the year, more than a dozen antique shops also lure visitors. A list of these stores is available at the information gazebo.

Albany's **World Championship Timber Carnival** (541/928-2391) takes place July 1–4. While such events as speed-climbing, springboard-chopping, and log-rolling have little place in the increasingly mechanized world of modern timber management, they're still fun to watch.

Check www.albanyvisitors.com for more information about Albany events.

Accommodations and Food

Both Eugene and Corvallis are more lively places to stay, but if you're going to spend the night in Albany, it should be in an 1856 Victorian. The **Trainhouse Inn B&B** (206 7th Ave., 541/794-5281, www.trainhouseinn.com, $75 and up), located in the center of the historic district, fits the bill precisely. Don't worry that you'll be kept awake by railroad noise; the inn takes its name from Samuel Train, an early newspaper publisher.

At the **Albany Farmers Market** (Water Ave. and Broadalbin St., 9 A.M.–noon Sat., June–Thanksgiving) you can enjoy the Willamette

Valley's bountiful harvests of corn, fruit, garlic, peppers, or whatever else happens to be in season. Cut flowers are on sale as well as such regional specialties as the mild-tasting large-cloved elephant garlic, marionberries (a tart hybrid blackberry developed by Oregon State University), and dried jumbo Brooks prunes. Best of all, you're buying directly from the grower at a fraction of supermarket prices.

An Albany tradition is **Novak's Hungarian Restaurant** (2306 Heritage Way SE, 541/967-9488, 7 A.M.–9 P.M. daily, dinner $10–19). Authentic *kolbasz* (a spicy sausage), stuffed cabbage, and chicken paprika exemplify the earthy Eastern European fare served in a family-friendly atmosphere. A $15 Hungarian buffet is a good way to sample the food. Another local tradition is coffee and a pastry or light meal at **The Beanery** (1852 Fescue St. SE, 541/812-2500, 6 A.M.–7 P.M. Mon.–Sat., 7 A.M.–6 P.M. Sun., $3–9), located just off I-5.

Amtrak (110 W. 10th St., 541/928-0885) makes a stop in Albany. Greyhound no longer has a station here; the nearest is in Corvallis.

BROWNSVILLE

A down-home version of the pioneer experience awaits in Brownsville, which might evoke a feeling of déjà vu as it provided big-screen backdrops for a number of films, including *Stand By Me.* From I-5 take Exit 216; Route 228 will take you 5 miles east into this small town located between the Calapooia River and the Cascade foothills. What ended up being Oregon's third-oldest continuously operating settlement began as a ferry stop on the Calapooia River. This 1846 settlement began to prosper in 1862 with a woolen mill and, shortly thereafter, the coming of the railroad. Today, the **Linn County Historical Museum** (101 Park Ave., 541/466-3390, 11 A.M.–4 P.M. Mon.–Sat., 1–5 P.M. Sun., donation suggested) is located in a turn-of-the-20th-century train depot flanked by freight cars and a circus train. Inside these structures are displays (a barbershop, kitchen, post office, etc.) illustrating the lifestyle of the area's first settlers, the Kalapuya Native American people, and local natural history. Kids will especially relish the vintage covered wagon and 50 miniature horse-drawn wagons, sleighs, carriages, and carts.

Check at the museum about tours of the **Moyer House** (204 N. Main St.), the elegant 1881 Italianate home of a successful mill owner and door manufacturer. The home's high-ceilinged interior features a Carrara marble fireplace, ornate wood trim, hand-painted floral patterns, stencils on the ceilings, and oil-painted outdoor scenes on the upper panels of the bay windows. The 1881 grand piano in the south parlor is another must-see. The distinctive cupola perched atop the roof housing a glass observatory will catch your eye from a distance. Come in June to see the strangely twisted wisteria tree on the front lawn in full bloom.

The Brownsville area has other worthwhile attractions. A **pioneer cemetery** on the east end of Kirk Street shelters the grave of the last known member of the Kalapuya people; some headstones here date to 1846, when Brownsville was established. A collection of rocks, Native American arrowheads, and woodcarvings is housed in an interesting stone structure at the **Living Rock Studio** (911 W. Bishop Way, 541/466-5814, 10 A.M.–5 P.M. Tues.–Sat., $3 suggested donation). The highlight is the series of colorful Biblical scenes made from thin slabs of rock, but don't miss out on the second-floor logging exhibit. The Sweet Home area (about 17 miles east of Brownsville) is famous among rock hounds for petrified wood and agates.

The historical museum coordinates wagon-ride interludes into the past during the first weekend of May. Known as **Carriage Me Back Days,** these excursions reenact daily life from days of old.

The third weekend in June, the 100-year-old **Brownsville Pioneer Picnic** features an old-time fiddlers jamboree and a tug-of-war involving large local teams. Also on the agenda are a parade, a carnival, a crafts fair, a foot race, and a tour of historical homes. The three-day celebration is held near the spot where a ferry plied the Calapooia in 1846, now part of 10-acre Pioneer Park, located off Main Street at the end of Park Avenue. Each day of the event begins with a wagon-train breakfast.

Another event of interest is the **Antique Fair** on the first weekend of August, where food, entertainment, and treasures from old farmsteads are featured.

In the past couple of years, the event that has drawn the biggest crowds to Brownsville is the late-August **Willamette Country Music Festival** (541/497-7588, www. willamettecountrymusicfest.com), with lots of music and camping.

Should you decide to overnight in the Brownsville area, you can get a room at **Pioneer Best Western Lodge** (33180 Hwy. 228, 541/369-2804, $77 and up), located at the intersection of I-5 and Route 228. There's also a campground in Brownsville's Pioneer Park (541/466-5666, $10 tents, $15 RVs) near the Calapooia River.

Eugene

Eugene's location confers many blessings. The Willamette River curves around the northwest quarter of the community (pop. about 150,000), and abundant trees and flowers dot the cityscape. From an elevated perch you can see the Coast and Cascade Ranges beckoning you to beach and mountain playgrounds little more than an hour away.

In town, a world-renowned Bach Festival and other big-time cultural events are showcased in the Hult Center, praised by the *Los Angeles Times* as having the best acoustics on the West Coast. The University of Oregon campus provides another forum for the best in art and academe, while its Hayward Field track has been the site of the U.S. Olympic Trials several times.

Outdoor gatherings such as Saturday Market and the Oregon Country Fair bring the community together in a potlatch of homegrown edibles, arts, and crafts. But it doesn't take an organized festival to draw the townsfolk outside. Even during persistent winter rains, locals can be seen jogging, bicycling, and gardening.

For residents of the sparsely populated hamlets east, west, and south of town, Eugene is a hub for health care and shopping. Visitors from rural Lane County flock to the Eugene-Springfield area on weekends to shop at Valley River Center, see a movie, attend a convention, or simply go "garage saling."

Eugene's labor, environmental, and human services organizations have labored with quiet effectiveness for several decades, giving the town a distinct lefty touch with worker-owned collectives, a wheelchair-friendly cityscape, preserved ancient forests, and wetland protection against industrial pollution.

As lovely as Eugene is, it might pose some problems for those with sensitive respiratory systems. Because of sporadic temperature inversions over the southern Willamette Valley, which is framed by mountain ranges that narrow like a funnel near the town, wintertime air stagnation is not uncommon. And the Eugene area, like most of the Willamette Valley, is notorious for its springtime pollens from ornamentals, trees, and grass-seed fields, making this season a challenge for the allergy sufferer.

Be that as it may, Eugene belongs on the itinerary of anyone who wants to experience a laid-back Northwest version of urban sophistication and active pursuits in a beautiful natural setting.

SIGHTS

Two major areas of interest to visitors are immediately south of the Willamette River. The campus, in Eugene's southeast quadrant, and the downtown (bounded by 5th and 10th Avenues and Charnelton and High Streets) are only a five-minute drive from each other. Serious walkers can manage the two-mile distance without trouble. Another excellent place to stroll, run, or bike with the locals, Alton

Baker Park, is just across the river from downtown and the university.

The major north–south thoroughfare is Willamette Street, which can be followed from downtown five miles south to Eugene's favorite hiking haunt, Spencer's Butte.

Skinner Butte

A good place to get oriented in Eugene, visually as well as historically, is Skinner Butte. If you look north from almost anywhere downtown, you'll see this landmark. A beautiful park fronting the Willamette River is located at the butte's northern base. This riverfront site served as a dock for pioneer sternwheelers and was where founding father Eugene Skinner ran a ferry service for farmers living north of the river. The town tried to become a major shipping port, but the upper Willamette was uncharted as well as too shallow and meandering. In addition, sunken logs, gravel bars, and submerged trees and rocks made steamboat navigation difficult. As a result, Ben Holladay's Oregon and California Railroad became Eugene's most effective mode of transport in 1871.

Eugene Skinner, like so many Oregon Trail–era migrants, wanted to take advantage of the federal government's 320-acre land giveaway offer to pioneers, so he staked a claim from the banks of the Willamette to present-day 8th Avenue and from Monroe Street to the river on Hilyard Street. He built his shelter at 2nd Avenue and Lincoln Street and later opened up Lane County's first trading post.

From downtown, head north on High Street, which becomes Cheshire Avenue as it curves to the left. Take a left onto Skinner Butte Loop and follow it to the top. You can also get here by traveling north on Lincoln Street to Skinner Butte Loop or by walking up from the south side, which takes about 15 minutes. From the top of the butte, enjoy the vantage point from which Eugene Skinner surveyed the landscape in June 1846. Kalapuyas called this promontory Yapoah, meaning "high place," and used it for ceremonial dances. Despite the state's second most concentrated population, which has

© JUDY JEWELL

Skinner Butte rises above downtown Eugene. Head to the top to orient yourself to the city.

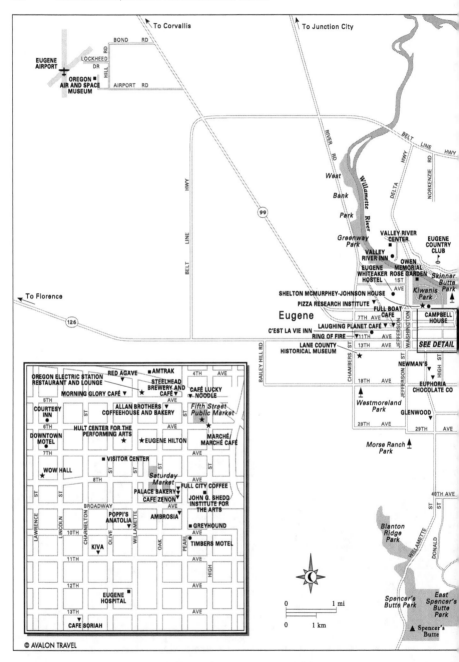

To Corvallis

To Junction City

EUGENE AIRPORT

OREGON AIR AND SPACE MUSEUM

BOND   RD
LOCKHEED DR
HILL RD
AIRPORT   RD

99

BELT LINE HWY

RIVER RD

NORKENZIE RD

DELTA HWY

West

Bank

Park

Willamette River

Greenway Park

VALLEY RIVER CENTER

EUGENE COUNTRY CLUB

VALLEY RIVER INN

EUGENE WHITEAKER HOSTEL

OWEN MEMORIAL ROSE GARDEN
1ST AVE

Skinner Butte Park

Kiwanis Park

SHELTON MCMURPHEY-JOHNSON HOUSE

PIZZA RESEARCH INSTITUTE

Eugene

C'EST LA VIE INN

FULL BOAT CAFE

7TH AVE

LAUGHING PLANET CAFÉ

RING OF FIRE   11TH AVE

LANE COUNTY HISTORICAL MUSEUM   13TH AVE

CAMPBELL HOUSE

JEFFERSON

WASHINGTON

SEE DETAIL

To Florence

126

BAILEY HILL RD

CHAMBERS ST

NEWMAN'S

18TH AVE

Westmoreland Park

28TH AVE

HIGH ST

JEFFERSON

EUPHORIA CHOCOLATE CO

GLENWOOD

29TH AVE

Morse Ranch Park

OREGON ELECTRIC STATION RESTAURANT AND LOUNGE

RED AGAVE

AMTRAK

4TH   AVE

MORNING GLORY CAFÉ

STEELHEAD BREWERY AND CAFÉ

CAFÉ LUCKY NOODLE

5TH

COURTESY INN

ALLAN BROTHERS COFFEEHOUSE AND BAKERY

AVE

Fifth Street Public Market

6TH

DOWNTOWN MOTEL

HULT CENTER FOR THE PERFORMING ARTS

EUGENE HILTON

AVE

MARCHÉ/ MARCHÉ CAFÉ

7TH

VISITOR CENTER

AVE

WOW HALL

8TH

Saturday Market

AVE

PALACE BAKERY
CAFE ZENON

FULL CITY COFFEE

JOHN G. SHEDD INSTITUTE FOR THE ARTS

BROADWAY

POPPI'S ANATOLIA

AMBROSIA

AVE

GREYHOUND

10TH

KIVA

TIMBERS MOTEL

AVE

11TH

AVE

LAWRENCE ST

LINCOLN ST

CHARNELTON ST

OLIVE ST

WILLAMETTE ST

OAK ST

PEARL ST

HIGH

12TH

AVE

EUGENE HOSPITAL

13TH

AVE

CAFE SORIAH

40TH AVE

WILLAMETTE ST

DONALD ST

Blanton Ridge Park

Spencer's Butte Park

East Spencer's Butte Park

Spencer's Butte

0   1 mi
0   1 km

© AVALON TRAVEL

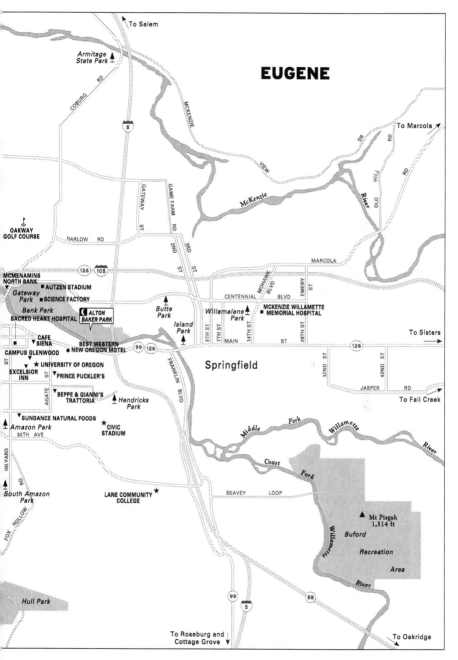

EUGENE

grown in the once-pristine southern Willamette Valley below, on a clear day you can still see the Cascade and Coast Ranges as well as pockets of greenery throughout the city. You can also spot another good reference point in your orientation, **Spencer's Butte,** looming above the southern hills four miles away.

In the Skinner Butte area don't miss the 1888 **Shelton McMurphey-Johnson House** (303 Willamette St., 541/484-0808, www. smjhouse.org, 10 A.M.–1 P.M. Tues.–Fri., 1–4 P.M. Sat.–Sun., tours weekends and occasional weekdays, $5 adults, $2 children 12 and under) on the lower south slope of the butte. The aqua-colored Victorian is the most eye-catching of some 2,000 designated historic properties in the city.

Owen Rose Garden

Near the base of Skinner Butte and along the banks of the Willamette, the thirty varieties of roses at the Owen Rose Garden (300 N. Jefferson St., 541/682-4824, open daily) peak in June and bloom until fall. Along with 4,500 roses and magnolia blossoms in spring, tremendous old cherry and oak trees also command attention. To get here from I-5, take I-105 West and take the West Eugene off-ramp. Turn right at the bottom of the ramp onto Madison Street and follow it north toward the Willamette River. One block to your right is Jefferson Street and the entrance to the Rose Garden. A more pleasant approach is on foot, via the riverside bike path behind the Valley River Inn (ask at the front desk for directions) until you get to the footbridge. On the other side of the river, loop back in the direction of the hotel for about 0.5 miles until you arrive at the rose garden.

Fifth Street Public Market

The past and the present happily coexist a few blocks from the butte's south flank at the Fifth Street Public Market (296 E. 5th Ave.), an old-time feed mill converted into an atrium. This rustic structure houses an impressive collection of specialty stores and restaurants surrounding an open-air courtyard. This courtyard is a favorite haunt of sun worshippers, people-watchers, and street performers. Note: Although the market bears the word *street* in its name, it is actually located on East 5th Avenue and High Street.

Eugene Saturday Market

For a more down-home version of the public market, explore the crafts, food, and street performances at the Saturday Market (8th Ave. and Oak St., 541/686-8885, www.eugenesaturdaymarket.org, 10 A.M.–5 P.M. Sat. Apr.–mid-Nov.); the good vibes and creative spirit of the community are in ample evidence. The market moves indoors to the Lane County Fairgrounds (13th Ave. and Jefferson St.) to become the Holiday Market from the weekend before Thanksgiving through Christmas Eve (open Sat.–Sun. and some weekdays).

The small farmers market (9 A.M.–4 P.M. Sat. Apr.–mid-Nov. and 10 A.M.–3 P.M. Tues. May–Oct.) set up across 8th Avenue from the crafts area is a good place to get fresh produce.

Hult Center for the Performing Arts

While you're walking between the two markets, you might look west past the Eugene Hilton and notice another imposing building close by. This is the Hult Center for the Performing Arts (1 Eugene Center, Willamette St. between 6th Ave. and 7th Ave., 541/687-5000, www.hultcenter.org). In addition to its status as a topflight performance venue, this place is worth a look for its aesthetics alone. From the frog and troll statues that greet you at the 6th Avenue entrance to the high-ceilinged interior bedecked with masks, artistic touches abound.

Hult Center talent (with nine resident companies) is showcased beneath interlocking acoustic panels on the domed ceiling and walls of the 2,500-seat **Silva Concert Hall** (which resembles a giant upside-down pastel-colored Easter basket). The **Jacobs Gallery** exhibits local artwork, providing another feast for the eyes. Even the bathroom tile is done up in a visually pleasing theatrical motif. Free one-hour guided tours are offered every other Thursday at noon or by special arrangement. Call 541/682-5733 to check the schedule.

University of Oregon Campus

From downtown, head a few blocks south to 13th Avenue, then east to the University of Oregon campus (visitor information available at Oregon Hall, Agate St. and 13th Ave., 541/346-3111, www.uoregon.edu), bounded by Franklin Boulevard, 11th and 18th Avenues, and Alder and Moss Streets. With an enrollment of over 20,000 students, you might be expecting a bureaucratic, impersonal feeling; instead the grounds of the campus are graced by architecturally inviting buildings dating back to the school's creation in the 1870s, as well as 400 varieties of trees.

Deady Hall, the oldest building on campus, was built in 1876. Also noteworthy are two museums on campus: the Jordan Schnitzer Museum of Art and the Natural History

The University of Oregon campus has some lovely old trees and a couple of good museums.

Museum. The quiet and tranquility of the campus are sustained by a ban on vehicular traffic beyond 13th Avenue and Kincaid Street. A free **campus tour** leaves from Oregon Hall weekdays at 9:30 A.M. and 12:30 P.M. and Saturdays at 10:30 A.M. But unless you're a prospective student, you're better off just picking up the map and setting your own pace.

Across from the Schnitzer Museum of Art is the **University of Oregon Library.** On the second floor, the **Oregon Collection** (541/346-3468) has books and periodicals about the state in open stacks—a great place to plan trips or learn about the region. The nationally famous map library on the first floor can also augment the trip-planning process with its extensive collection of all sorts of maps, its helpful staff, and its well-tuned photocopying machines.

This campus has often been selected by Hollywood to portray the ivy-covered halls of academe, most notably in the comedy *Animal House.*

If you wander the north part of the University of Oregon complex toward Franklin Boulevard, you'll see majestic and rare trees (including a Chinese dawn redwood) dotting the landscape between the law and journalism schools. Interesting outdoor sculptures also liven up a stroll on the campus.

Museums

A must on any campus tour is the recently renovated and expanded **Jordan Schnitzer Museum of Art** (next to the main library, 1430 Johnson Lane, 541/346-3027, http://uoma.uoregon.edu, 11 A.M.–5 P.M. Tues. and Thurs.–Sun., 11 A.M.–8 P.M. Wed. year-round, $5 adults, $3 seniors, ages 18 and under free). This museum is a real gem, with a surprisingly good collection of contemporary art, including works by Chuck Close, Mark Tobey, Morris Graves, and many Northwest artists. Another major highlight is a nationally renowned Asian collection (don't miss the jade); the revolving paintings and photography exhibits on the first floor are also usually worthwhile.

The university's other quite wonderful museum is entirely different: The **Natural**

History Museum (1680 E. 15th Ave., 541/346-3024, www.uoregon.edu/~mnh, 11 A.M.–5 P.M. Wed.–Sun., $3, $2 students and seniors) showcases Oregon's prehistory and includes artifacts from digs in eastern Oregon as well as bird and mammal fossils from around the state. A portion of Thomas Condon's fossil collection displays the curiosities culled from the earth by the man known as Oregon's first geologist and the discoverer of the John Day Fossil Beds. There's also a set of sagebrush sandals dated at 9,350 years old (from the collection of those found by Dr. Luther Cressman), 15-million-year-old shell fossils, a whale vertebra, and mammoth tusks. To get there from Hayward Field on Agate Street, go east on 15th Avenue and look for a fish sculpture on your right, in front of an attractive wooden building, across the street from the dorms. Pick up the *Trees of Eugene* tour pamphlet at the information desk to annotate a scenic and historic jaunt through Eugene's leafy glades.

Maude Kerns Art Center (1910 E. 15th Ave., 541/345-1571, www.mkartcenter.org, 10 A.M.–5:30 P.M. Mon.–Fri., noon–4 P.M. Sat., free) is just east of the University of Oregon campus. Set in an old church, this gallery is dedicated to contemporary art of nationally known as well as regionally prominent artists. This gallery and others downtown are the focal points of a gallery walk (Lane Arts Council, 541/485-2278, www.lanearts.org, 5:30–8:30 P.M. first Fri. of the month).

Just across the river in Alton Baker Park **Science Factory** (2300 Leo Harris Pkwy., 541/682-7888, www.sciencefactory.org, 10 A.M.–4 P.M. daily summer, 10 A.M.–4 P.M. Wed.–Sun. during the school year, closed on university home football game days, $7 exhibits and planetarium, $4 exhibits or planetarium alone) is designed to stimulate scientific understanding and curiosity in everyday life. The permanent exhibits are similar to those at Portland's Oregon Museum of Science and Industry and are complemented by a new set of traveling exhibits every three months. The Science Factory's hands-on orientation reaches its apex during the summer.

The museum's excellent **planetarium** is highly recommended (shows 1 P.M. and 2 P.M. Sat.–Sun., $4). The Science Factory–Planetarium complex is reached from I-5 by taking I-105 West to the Coburg Road Exit and following the signs to Autzen Stadium (look for Centennial Boulevard and the Leo Harris Parkway).

The **Lane County Historical Museum** (740 W. 13th Ave., 541/682-4242, www.museumslanecounty.org, 10 A.M.–4 P.M. Wed.–Fri., noon–4 P.M. Sat.–Sun., $2 adults, $1 seniors, $0.75 youth) can be found next to the fairgrounds. Just look for the steam donkey on the front lawn. There are other 19th-century logging vehicles and period rooms on display. The Oregon Trail exhibits are among the most interesting.

Close to the Eugene Airport, the **Oregon Air and Space Museum** (90377 Boeing Dr., 541/461-1101, www.oasm.info, noon–4 P.M. Wed.–Sun., $5) has vintage aircraft, artifacts, and displays; serious aircraft buffs should visit McMinnville's air museum.

PARKS AND TRAILS

If you're looking for what makes Eugene Eugene, you'll get some pretty big clues by visiting the city's parks. Especially appealing and easy to get to is the **Willamette River Bike Trail,** a six-mile pathway running east–west on both sides of the river that takes in parts of Skinner Butte Park and Alton Baker Park.

◖ Alton Baker Park

Just across the Willamette River from downtown, the 400-acre Alton Baker Park is home to a world-class running trail, the Science Factory–Planetarium complex, gardens, ponds, picnic areas, a canoe canal, and part of a very cool scale model of the solar system (the sun and inner planets are here; Pluto, even though it's no longer considered a planet, is 3.66 miles to the northwest, along the bike path). The western part of the park is more developed; to the east it includes the 237-acre Whilamut Natural Area.

© PAUL LEVY

Eugene's riverside trails are great, and the Peter DeFazio footbridge connects Alton Baker Park with downtown.

The four-mile **Pre's Trail** runs along the Willamette River east of Alton Baker Park. Named after runner Steve Prefontaine, whose world-record times and finishing kicks used to rock the Hayward Field grandstands before his untimely death in a car accident in 1975, this soft path meanders along the river and connects to the network of trails along the Willamette.

Reach Alton Baker Park from downtown by taking the Ferry Street Bridge and turning right just after crossing the river; if you're on foot, the Peter DeFazio footbridge is right by the Ferry Street Bridge and is an easy walk from the Fifth Street Market area. From the U. of O. area, walk or bike across the Autzen Bike Bridge to the park.

Hendricks Park

About two miles east of the campus on a forested ridgeline is Hendricks Park (541/682-5324), home to 850 naturally occurring rhododendrons and azaleas and about 10,000 hybrids. There are several ways to get to the park, the easiest being to turn from Fairmount Boulevard onto Summit Drive. Or take Lane Transit Bus 27 for Fairmount, disembark at Summit Drive, and hike on up the hill 0.25 miles. Two parking lots accommodate cars—one near the picnic area of stoves and tables, the other at the upper entrance on Sunset Boulevard. The rhododendron gardens are in their glory during May, with 15–20-foot specimens in shades of pink, red, yellow, and purple. Even though the display declines by late June, it's always a great place to stroll. Gorgeous views of the city can be enjoyed from the west end of the garden, and tree-shaded footpaths lead to benches located in secluded cul-de-sacs on the hillside.

Ridgeline Trail

The South Hills Ridgeline Trail is only minutes from downtown Eugene and offers wildlife-watching opportunities (look for deer, tree frogs, garter snakes, and all kinds of birds) and more species of fern than perhaps any other single spot in Oregon. In addition, old-growth

KENTUCKY FALLS

Along with the well-known hiking areas described in this chapter, the nearby Coast Range has some hidden gems, thanks, paradoxically, to such extractive industries as logging and gravel. The industrial "cat" trails that once cut swaths through these forests are today maintained (and sometimes paved over) by the Forest Service for access to natural wonders. One such place is Kentucky Falls.

Picturesque **Kentucky Falls** (www.fs.fed.us/r6/siuslaw) is set in an old-growth forest on the upper slopes of the Coast Range. From downtown Eugene, drive 35 miles west on Route 126 to the Whittaker Creek Recreation Area on the south side of the road, approximately six miles west of the Walton Store and post office. The route to Kentucky Falls winds through the clear-cut lower slopes of 3,700-foot-high **Roman Nose Mountain.**

From Whittaker Creek Recreation Area, drive one mile south and make a right turn. After one mile, bear left on Dunn Ridge Road (Forest Service Rd. 18-8-28). After about seven miles the pavement ends, and you'll turn left on Knowles Creek Road; go 2.7 miles. Make a right onto Forest Service Road 23 (gravel) and proceed 1.6 miles until you make a right onto Forest Service Road 919. Continue for 2.6 miles to the Kentucky Falls trailhead, marked by a sign on the left side of the road. An old-growth Douglas fir forest on gently rolling hills for the first 0.5 miles gives way to a steep descent into a lush canyon. The upper waterfall is visible a little more than a mile down the trail. You'll hear the water before you actually get a full cross-section of a broad cascade pouring over the rim of the green canyon. On your drive back to Route 126, retrace your route carefully to avoid veering off on a hair-raising spur route to Mapleton.

Douglas fir and the lovely and increasingly hard-to-find calypso orchid grow here. The trail is seldom steep and has some spectacular views of the city through clearings. A spur route leads up to the highest point in Eugene, 2,052-foot Spencer's Butte, via a steep and often muddy trail. The Ridgeline Trail can be reached from several points, including Dillard Road; near the corner of Fox Hollow and Christenson Roads; near Willamette and 52nd; off Blanton Road near 40th; and the Spencer's Butte parking area.

Spencer's Butte

According to one legend, the butte was named after a 19th-century English trapper killed by Native American arrows. The Kalapuyans called it Chamate, meaning "rattlesnake mountain." An 1848 account (from Batterns DeGuerre's *Ten Years in Oregon*) of the view from the summit reads as follows:

On one hand was the vast chain of Cascade Mountains, Mount Hood looming in solitary grandeur far above its fellows; on the other hand was the Umpqua Mountains, and a little farther on, the coast ridge. Between these lay the whole magnificent panorama of the Willamette Valley, with its ribbon streams and carpetlike verdure.

The view today has all of the above, but there are some differences. Below the north summit you look down on Eugene-Springfield, with Fern Ridge Reservoir in the northwest toward Junction City. Beyond the reservoir you can sometimes see Mary's Peak. Other Cascade Mountains not noted in the previous account but sometimes visible from the butte include Mount Jefferson, Mount Washington, the Three Sisters, and Mount Bachelor. To the southeast, Creswell and the hills around Cottage Grove are visible.

The two main trails to the top vary in difficulty. If you bear left immediately after leaving the parking lot, you'll come to the route known among the locals as the Face. This trail is shorter in distance than its saddleback counterpart but is much steeper and is littered with boulders and sometimes muddy spots.

It can be scaled in 40 minutes by reasonably fit hikers.

The main trail is a straight shot from the parking lot, looping up and around the steep hills. These inclines are broken up by flat stretches. Allow about an hour for the ascent. Signs caution against rattlesnakes, falling limbs, and poison oak, the latter being the most likely problem. A mixed-conifer forest featuring old-growth Douglas fir with an understory of numerous ferns and wildflowers will usher you along.

The main parking lot for Spencer's Butte is on Willamette Street. Just drive south on Willamette Street until you see the signs on the left side of the road. There's also parking on Fox Hollow Road.

Mount Pisgah Arboretum

The Mount Pisgah Arboretum (Buford Park, 34901 Frank Parrish Rd., 541/747-3817) features seven miles of trails that pass through a number of different habitats. The arboretum at the end of Seavey Loop Road (plant and bird lists are often available at the visitors center, open weekends) sponsors such events as a fall fair dedicated to area mushrooms and a spring wildflower show and plant sale (dates vary; call ahead). Mount Pisgah can be reached by following East 30th Avenue from Eugene past Lane Community College to the I-5 interchange. Cross the bridge over the interstate, turn left, and take the next right onto Seavey Loop Road. You'll cross the Coast Fork of the Willamette River and then turn left onto a gravel road (look for the Mount Pisgah signs) that leads to the trailhead; the arboretum is just beyond the parking lot.

The path to the 1,514-foot summit has few trees, enabling hikers to enjoy vistas of the Willamette Valley on the way up. At the top an unforgettable perspective of the valley in the foreground and the Three Sisters and other Cascade peaks in the distance awaits. At the summit is a monument honoring author Ken Kesey's son and other members of the University of Oregon wrestling team who perished in a van accident (Oregon's most celebrated author lived two miles to the east in Pleasant Hill). This memorial consists of a sculpture with a relief map depicting the mountains, rivers, towns, and other landmarks in the Eugene area. Supporting the map are three five-sided bronze columns upon which the geologic history of Oregon over the past 200 million years is portrayed, using images of more than 300 fossil specimens.

Those making the climb in August will find blackberry bushes for browsing along the way. If you're perspiring from the climb, when you're back on the valley floor head south of the trailhead to the adjoining **Buford Recreation Area** for a dip in the cool waters of the Willamette River. The banks of the Coast Fork here also have a great profusion of white oak, blackberry bushes, and poison oak.

AROUND TOWN
Wineries

Right in town, you can visit the **Territorial Vineyards & Wine Company** winery (907 W. 3rd Ave., 541/684-9463, www.territorialvineyards.com, 5–9 p.m. Fri.–Sat.) to taste pinot noir, pinot gris, and Riesling.

LaVelle Vineyards (89697 Sheffler Rd., Elmira, 541/935-9406, www.lavellevineyards.com, noon–5 p.m. daily) makes a wonderful stop on the way out to the coast with a location just off Route 126 near Elmira. In addition to secluded tables with umbrellas at which to enjoy LaVelle's pinots and Rieslings with your picnic lunch, the works of local artists are on display in the winery itself. A trail to a hillside on the grounds lets you view the snowcapped Three Sisters on a clear day. The winery is also represented by a wine bar in the Fifth Street Market.

Silvan Ridge/Hinman Vineyards (27012 Briggs Hill Rd., 541/345-1945, www.silvanridge.com, noon–5 p.m. daily), 15 miles southwest of downtown near Crow, is a perfect place to spend a summer afternoon. Drive west on 11th Avenue, turn left on Bertelson Road, then right on Spencer Creek Road. A left down Briggs Hill Road takes you to the tasting room, located on a hillside overlooking a valley. The ride out is a favorite of local bicyclists, many of whom typically continue on into the Coast Range via Vaughan Road (ask for directions at the winery for the Crow Valley Store that sits opposite Vaughan Road). While at the vineyard, ask to sample Hinman's award-winning Gewürztraminer; the pinot gris is also delightful.

The lavish **King Estate Winery** (80854 Territorial Rd., 541/942-9874 or 800/884-4441, www.kingestate.com, noon–5 P.M. daily) is set on 820 acres with a state-of-the-art winery resembling a European château. Production focuses on organically grown pinot gris and pinot noir. In addition to wine, you can also sit down to a meal at the restaurant (541/685-5189, 11 A.M.–9 P.M. daily, dinner $22–32, reservations recommended). To reach the winery from Eugene, take I-5 South to Exit 182 (Creswell), turn west on Oregon Avenue (which becomes Camas Swale Rd. and then Ham Rd.) to Territorial Highway. Turn left onto Territorial Highway and follow it about 2.5 miles to King Estate.

Cottage Grove

The town of Cottage Grove, some 20 miles south of Eugene, is known for its covered bridges (there are six in the area; find excellent details at www.oregon.gov/odot/hwy/bridge/covered_bridges.shtml) and as being the gateway to the **Bohemia mining district,** site of old abandoned mines. Check the **Cottage Grove Pioneer Museum** (Birch Ave. and H St., 541/942-3963) for more information on these attractions, or contact the **Cottage Grove Chamber of Commerce** (710 E. Gibbs Ave., 541/942-2411, www.cgchamber.com), located 2 miles east of the ranger station in Cottage Grove. Ask also about the 14.1-mile **Row River Trail,** a rails-to-trails route that follows the paved-over tracks of an old mining train from Cottage Grove to Culp Creek—perfect for mountain biking, birding, and mushroom hunting (especially after the first fall rains). For more information on this route, contact the Bureau of Land Management, Eugene District (2890 Chad Dr., 541/683-6600).

SPORTS AND RECREATION

Eugene's identity is rooted in its reputation as "Tracktown, USA," and also in its superlative Parks and Recreation Department, miles of bike paths and on-street bike lanes, and back-country cycling minutes from downtown.

Water Recreation

Alton Baker Park, along the Willamette River, and the **Millrace Canal,** which parallels the river for three or four miles, provide escapes from Eugene's main downtown thoroughfares. The canal is easily accessed from the University of Oregon campus by crossing Franklin Boulevard. Farther west on the Willamette, near Skinner Butte and the Owen Rose Garden, is the **Riverhouse Outdoor Program** office (301 N. Adams St., 541/682-5329), headquarters of the Parks Department outdoor program and a roped-off swimming area. This is the place to rent river craft.

Reservoirs beyond downtown Eugene provide a wide range of recreation. The one closest to town is **Fern Ridge Lake.** Camp, picnic, swim, water-ski, sail, or watch wildlife. In addition, fishing for crappie, cutthroat trout, largemouth black bass, and catfish is excellent in early spring. This lake was formed when the Long Tom River was dammed in 1941, and its southeast shore was designated a wildlife refuge in 1979.

To reach the lake, drive 10 miles west of downtown on West 11th Avenue (Rte. 126) toward Veneta, or take Clear Lake Road off Route 99W. Sailboaters and sailboarders launch from marinas on the north and south shores. The lake is drained in winter to allow for flood control, but the resulting marsh and wildlife refuge host tree frogs, newts, ospreys, rare purple martins (in spring), black-tailed deer, red foxes, beavers, muskrats, minks, pond turtles, and great blue herons. The wildlife area is closed to the public January–March 15 for the protection of wintering birds. There are 250 species of birds found here, including tundra swans, northern harriers, Canada geese, mergansers, peregrine falcons, and egrets, which, with their white plumage, long legs, and large size are spectacularly easy to identify. To get here, make a right off Route 126 onto Territorial Road and look for a sign on the right. This section of Territorial Road is also part of the Old Applegate Trail, the southern counterpart to the Oregon Trail. This trail ended in the Salem area after coming up through Northern California into Oregon.

Dorena Reservoir, 50 minutes south of Eugene, has camping, fishing, and boating. The Army Corps dammed the Row River to create the reservoir, which can be reached by driving south on I-5 or Route 99 for 20 miles to Cottage Grove. Then head under the bridge below I-5's Cottage Grove Exit (Exit 174) and pick up Row River Road (it goes up into the mountains, so check snow conditions), which goes 8 miles east to Dorena Lake. Several miles up Row River Road, pick up Layng Road and go 1.5 miles to Currin Bridge, one of the area's six covered bridges. Another 1.2 miles south down Layng Road is Mosby Creek Bridge.

A popular retreat for locals is **Cougar Reservoir and Terwilliger Hot Springs.** From Eugene, go 42 miles on Route 126 to the town of Blue River, then 4 miles down Forest Service Road 19 (the paved Aufderheide Drive) up to the west side of Cougar Reservoir. The springs can be reached by hiking to the end of a short trail; thanks to user fees, they have remained a splendidly kept site. This trail overlooks a steep drop-off, so be careful. The several pools in this tranquil forest setting can be crowded on weekends. Purchase a Forest Service Recreation Pass at the trailhead or risk a fine.

Sports Facilities and Programs
Go for a swim in the indoor pools at **Echo Hollow** (1560 Echo Hollow Rd., 541/682-5525) or **Sheldon** (2445 Willakenzie Rd., 541/682-5314). Drop-in visitors pay a few bucks.

Lane County Ice (Lane County Fairgrounds, 796 W. 13th Ave., 541/687-3615) offers ice-skating lessons and open public skating.

It must be said that Eugene's weather sometimes makes indoor activities more appealing than scampering up wet rocks. On those days,

or after a day of running and biking, drop in for some yoga at **Four Winds Center** (in the Tamarack Wellness Center, 3575 Donald St., 541/484-6100, www.fourwindsyoga.org), which offers a wide variety of classes with some very good teachers.

Of the many public **tennis** courts throughout Eugene, the best-lit facilities are at the University of Oregon and at 24th Avenue and Amazon Parkway near Roosevelt Middle School.

Hiking and Biking
Near the Amazon courts, runners will enjoy the bark-o-mulch trail that follows Amazon Creek in a 1-mile loop. Of course, the best jogging is along **Pre's Trail** along the Willamette River east of Alton Baker Park. Another good route is the road behind 24-Hour Fitness (1475 Franklin Blvd.), which is closed to motorized traffic. This leads to a footbridge that takes bikers, hikers, and joggers to Pre's Trail, the Willamette River Bike Trail, Autzen Stadium, and other facilities found along the Willamette River Greenway.

Eugene and Springfield together boast 120 miles of on-street bike lanes, limited-access streets, and off-street bikeways. The two cities collaborate to publish a free bicycle map; find it online by going to the Eugene city website (www.eugene-or.gov) and searching for "bicycle map." **Collins Cycle Shop** (60 E. 11th Ave., 541/342-4878) is centrally located. Here and elsewhere, look for the high-quality bikes, bike equipment, backpacks, and raingear made by the local **Burley Designs** co-op. Another innovative local bike business is **Bike Friday** (541/687-0487 or 888/777-0258, www.bike-friday.com), known for their extra-cool custom-made folding bicycles.

Spectator Sports
Each spring, the University of Oregon track team, a perennial contender for the status of best team in the nation, holds meets at **Hayward Field** (Agate St. and 15th Ave.). This site has also hosted such world-class events as the National Collegiate Athletic

Association Finals and the United States Olympic Trials.

Fall means Duck football at **Autzen Stadium** (Martin Luther King Blvd. on Day Island). To get there, head north on Ferry Street; just after crossing the Willamette River, take a hard right on Martin Luther King Boulevard. In winter, the townsfolk cram into **MacArthur Court,** a funky anachronism from the 1920s located just south of the physical education building on University Street. Even if you're not a fan, you're bound to get caught up in the frenzied decibels of "quacker backers" who support a team known for its never-say-die attitude.

In summer, the **Eugene Emeralds** play ball at Civic Stadium (2077 Willamette St., 541/342-5367), for honor, glory, and a chance to break into the big leagues. Even if you don't catch a future hall-of-famer on the way up, enjoy the best concession food you'll ever taste at a ballpark.

Golf

Laurelwood Golf Course (2700 Columbia St., 541/484-4653 for tee times) is a city-owned golf course with a 250-yard driving range. Greens fees ($25) and rentals are reasonable.

Of the many courses in Lane County, **Tokatee** (54947 Rte. 126, Blue River, 541/822-3220 or 800/452-6376, $42 for 18 holes) is the best. To get there, drive 47 miles east of Eugene on the McKenzie Highway (Rte. 126). The 18 holes are set in a mountainous landscape patrolled by elk and other forest creatures in the shadow of the Three Sisters.

Climbing

Some of the best urban climbing to be found anywhere is at the Columns, a basalt cliff located on public land against the west side of Skinner Butte in downtown Eugene. Limited parking is available at the Columns, but it's more enjoyable to ride a bike here by following the road rimming the butte. Climbing is free.

ENTERTAINMENT

Keeping up with Eugene's multifaceted entertainment offerings involves previewing the listings put out by two local newspapers, *Eugene Weekly* (http://eugeneweekly.com) and the daily *Eugene Register Guard* (www.registerguard.com); both have good online events listings, with the *Weekly* being a little more alternative. Call the University of Oregon ticket office (541/346-4461) for athletic event information. For more information on what's happening around town, peruse the community bulletin boards at Fifth Street Public Market and Sundance Natural Foods.

Dancing and Music

If you tire of watching other folks in action, the best spot for frenetic dancing in town is the **W.O.W. Hall** (291 W. 8th Ave., 541/687-2746, www.wowhall.org). This old Wobblie (International Workers of the World) meeting hall has remained a monument to Oregon's activist past in labor history (well, sort of, anyway: Its motto is now "Fighting to save rock & roll since 1975"). Despite having all the ambience of a junior-high-school gym, it hosts some surprisingly famous rock and blues performers. The W.O.W. bills itself as having the best hardwood dance floor in the Pacific Northwest. In any case, it's probably the most crowded and features an interesting cross section of Eugenians. Beer and wine are served downstairs.

The **John G. Shedd Institute for the Arts** (868 High St., 541/434-7000, www.theshedd.org) brings in some really fun music (think Buckwheat Zydeco, Dar Williams, Steve Martin playing his banjo) and offers a wide variety of programs, including a performing arts company, a cultural arts center, and a community music school. Concerts are at the Shedd's Jaqua Concert Hall, the Hult Center, and other locations.

Dancing to live bands at the **Erb Memorial Union Ballroom** (13th Ave. and University St., 541/346-6000) is a Eugene tradition. Local guy who made good Robert Cray and other nationally known performers have played here. The dance floor is more spacious than the W.O.W. Hall's but can actually exceed its downtown counterpart in BTUs generated by the mass of writhing bodies.

Concerts frequently take place within the cavernous enclaves of Autzen Stadium, the home field to the Oregon Ducks football team. A good sound system has made it possible for tens of thousands of concert attendees to enjoy such artists as Bob Dylan and U2.

For more sedate listening, the **Hult Center** is next door to the Hilton. The Eugene Symphony and other estimable local groups like the Eugene Concert Choir perform here along with a wide-ranging array of headliners from the world of music and comedy. This is also where the Bach Festival concerts occur. At Christmastime, the Eugene Ballet's *Nutcracker* is always a treat.

The **Oregon Electric Station Restaurant and Lounge** (27 E. 5th Ave., 541/485-4444) hosts live jazz and is open nightly. This historic landmark features excellent dinner ($18–30) and lunch ($8–16) entrées, a full bar, a back room with wing chairs, and the ambience of an English club. But you never forget you're in Tracktown, USA, thanks to a wall festooned with photos of Alberto Salazar and Steve Prefontaine.

In the same neighborhood, **The Beanery** (152 W. 5th Ave., 541/342-3378) has live folk and blues at night and excellent coffee. This spacious coffeehouse, located in a charming old building across from the Lane County Jail, attracts everyone from off-duty cops to madmen playing speed chess. Home-baked goodies and breakfast, lunch, and dinner entrées (under $10) can be ordered at the counter. The Beanery is open every day.

Several clubs are clustered within about a two-block area around West Broadway. **John Henry's** (77 W. Broadway, 541/342-3358) is a music-oriented bar, with a bit of a punk touch. **Jameson's** (115 W. Broadway, 541/485-9913) has a good atmosphere; it's classy but not overly fussy. **SNAFU** (64 W. 8th Alley) is a gay-oriented dance bar with fancied-up discoball lighting.

Out in the Whiteaker neighborhood, **Sam Bond's Garage** (407 Blair Blvd., 541/343-2635) serves live music (including weekly bluegrass jams), microbrews, and a menu of vegetarian pub grub until dawn; it's open every day.

Theaters

While there's no shortage of movie houses in this town, the real screen gems are usually found at the university (consult the *Oregon Daily Emerald*, the U. of O. student newspaper, available free on and near campus) and the **Bijou Theatre** (492 E. 13th Ave., 541/686-2458, www.bijou-cinemas.com). The university series favors cult films and classics, and the inexpensive ticket price helps you forget the oppressiveness of the lecture halls that serve as theaters. For about twice the price, the Bijou is the place to see foreign films, art flicks, and less commercial mainstream movies. Located in an intimate Moorish-style converted church, the Bijou offers great munchies and late-night presentations.

Cutting-edge theater can be enjoyed at **Lord Leebrick** (540 Charnelton St., 541/684-6988).

EVENTS

There is a lot happening in this south Willamette Valley hub of culture and athletics. Several events, however, best impart the flavor of the area.

Oregon Bach Festival

Of all the kultur-fests in the Willamette Valley, only one enjoys international acclaim. The Oregon Bach Festival (541/346-5666 and 800/457-1486, www.oregonbachfestival.com) takes place over two weeks late June–early July under the baton of famed Bach interpreter Helmuth Rilling from Germany. The *New York Times* once rated the festival the best of its kind in the country, and an influx of renowned visiting opera and symphonic virtuosos guarantees that this will remain the case. More than two dozen separate concerts are featured, with musical styles ranging from the baroque era to the 20th century. The centerpieces of the festival, however, are Bach works such as the *St. Matthew Passion,* numerous cantatas, and the Brandenburg Concertos.

Performances take place in the Hult Center and at the Beall Concert Hall at the University of Oregon Music School. Free events, including "Let's Talk with the Conductor," miniconcerts, and children's activities also take place at these venues during the festival. Particularly recommended is the festival's Discovery Series: six concertos preceded by a short lecture-demo by Helmuth Rilling. Each 5 P.M. concert features a different Bach church cantata. Free noon concerts in the Hult lobby are also popular. A scheduled series of brunches, lunches, and dinners with the musicians also adds a special touch to the event.

Art and the Vineyard

Appealing to lowbrow and highbrow alike is Art and the Vineyard, which generally takes place over the Fourth of July weekend in Alton Baker Park. This event brings together art, music, and wine in a tranquil park near the Willamette River. One hundred artists' booths and the offerings of a dozen vineyards frequently grace the affair, along with live music (jazz, country, blues, and folk) and food concessions. Admission is charged to this outdoor celebration of Eugene's cultural richness. Contact the Maud Kerns Art Center (541/345-1571) for details and tickets.

Track Events

When Eugene hosted the 2008 U.S. Olympic team's track and field trials, town was booked up months in advance. If you are planning to visit around June 2012, book your room now; the Olympic trials will be here again.

Other Events

A gallery walk the first Friday of every month lets culture vultures enjoy open house exhibitions all over town. Consult the preceding Sunday's *Register Guard* for a complete listing of participating venues.

The university sponsors the **Willamette Valley Folk Festival** (541/686-INFO—541/686-4636) in May, which has attracted loosely defined folkies ranging from Tom Paxton to Doc Watson to Ani DiFranco. Call for a schedule of upcoming concerts. The free event is held in Alton Baker Park at the Cuthbert Amphitheatre; bring some cash to enjoy Eugene's amazing array of food vendors.

Music lovers also revel in the city's summer **Concerts in the Parks** festival. A series of free concerts is also held in Alton Baker Park's Cuthbert Amphitheatre mid-July–late August. Nancy Griffith, David Grisman, and Robert Cray typify the national names appearing. Call 541/687-5000 for tickets and information. Lower profile groups grace Amazon and Westmoreland Parks as well as several other venues throughout the city. Contact CVALCO (800/547-5445) for a schedule and more information.

Bohemia Mining Days (541/942-5064, www.bohemiaminingdays.org) convenes in mid-July; many of the events take place at re-created Bohemia City south of Eugene on Route 99 in Cottage Grove. Highlights of the four-day event include the Miner's Dinner and street dance, gold-panning demonstrations, and a carnival. Don't miss the Grand Miner's Parade, which happens on Saturday morning. Floats, horse teams, drill teams, and color guards make their way from Harrison Avenue to Row River Road with colorful costumes and the kind of enthusiasm last seen around here after turn-of-the-20th-century lucky strikes.

Also outside of Eugene, the annual **Junction City Scandinavian Festival** (Greenwood St. between 5th Ave. and 7th Ave., Junction City, www.scandinavianfestival.com) celebrates the town's Danish founders the second weekend in August. Swedish, Finnish, Norwegian, and Icelandic heritage also exert a presence at the festival. Folk dancing, traditional crafts, and food make up the bulk of the activities. Skits of Hans Christian Andersen folktales are enacted during the four-day event, along with

OREGON COUNTRY FAIR

Just after the Bach Festival in mid-July, the Oregon Country Fair takes place as the second major cultural event of the summer. If you didn't realize that there was still a thriving counterculture, buy a ticket online or at a Safeway store, put on your man-kilt, and catch a bus at the Valley River Mall for the fairgrounds along with the crowds of tie-dyed, fringed, and love-beaded fair-goers. Entering the fair, you wander through a kaleidoscope of natural fabrics, graceful ceramics, stained glass, rainbow candles, and thousands of other variously sculpted wares. Machine-manufactured items are simply unavailable. Every aspect of the fair – its 350-plus booths and its participants – is, in a sense, art.

What? Two hours gone by already? You need a cup of espresso and a piece of torte if you're going to make it through this day. Or perhaps you want a **Ritta's** burrito bulging with avocado, salsa, and sprouts. The choices are mouthwatering: Get fried rice, sushi, blazing salads, or even a tofu-less tofu burger (with 100 percent ground beef), and more.

Overwhelmed by the constant parade of costumed stilt walkers, strolling musicians, winged "country fairies," children in face paint, bare-breasted men and women, and other ambient wonders? Not far from any burnout point is a stage.

Shady Grove is a quiet venue for acoustic folk, classical, New Age, and other music. The **Daredevil, W. C. Fields,** and **Energy Park** stages host contemporary New Vaudeville stars and other rollicking performers. See the **Royale Famille du Canniveaux** debut a unique musical comedy. Marvel as the **Reduced Shakespeare Company** performs *Romeo and Juliet* backward in one minute flat. Shake your head and mutter as **Up For Grabs** juggles circular-saw blades and/or small children.

But wait, there's more. Try **The Circus** with its parade, orchestra, and veteran virtuosos. Ogle snake charmers and belly dancers at the **Gypsy Stage.** Or dance to the national and international stars of rock and roll, reggae, and alternative music on the **Main Stage.**

If it's starting to sound less like a hippie fair and more like a well-catered and established art convention, don't worry; there's always a sojourn into geo-socio-political-eco-consciousness at **Community Village.** Several booths here and in **Energy Park** teach and demonstrate the latest in new and matured '60s activism and environmental awareness.

Tired already? So are we, but there's a whole year to rest up and reminisce before the next Oregon Country Fair.

This annual fantasyland is staged among the trees east of Noti on Route 126. Take the free shuttle from Eugene's Valley River Mall directly to the wooded fair site near the Long Tom River, 13 miles from Eugene. Bus service usually begins at about 10:30 A.M., with the last departure from the fair site at 7 P.M. Due to the popularity of this event, which attracts more than 50,000 attendees, mandatory advance ticket purchase prior to your arrival on-site has been instituted for those taking mass transit. Car access to the fair is open 10 A.M.–6 P.M., but on-site parking is limited. Parking costs $7 at the gate, a couple of bucks less when reserved in advance.

For more information, contact the Oregon Country Fair (541/343-4298, www.oregoncountryfair.org). Admission is $18-26 (kids 10 and under free, 65 and over get a $5 discount). Purchase tickets in advance through **Tickets West** (800/992-8499, http://ticketswest.rdln. com). Dogs, drugs, glass containers, and video recorders are prohibited.

guided hour-long bus tours that take you by Scandinavian pioneer farmsteads. Junction City is 12 miles northwest of Eugene off Route 99. Another Junction City–area event is the mid-March Daffodil Drive, west of town at the Long Tom Grange.

Autumn is ushered in with the **Eugene Celebration** (541/681-4108, www.eugenecelebration.com, 3-day pass $12). This three-day fete in late September includes such events as three parades (one is a pet parade, another features bike lights), an art show, a jazz festival, and the coronation of the Slug Queen. Street performers all over town and food booths in the parking lot at 8th Avenue and Willamette Street also help the community put its best foot forward.

ACCOMMODATIONS

A few bed-and-breakfasts and a youth hostel provide the best value for the dollar in town, and there are plenty of inexpensive motels on East Broadway and moderately priced ones on Franklin Boulevard. (Before you check into one of these places, walk or drive a couple of blocks behind the motel toward the river just to make sure that the train tracks aren't too close—at 3 A.M. it can sound like trains are running right through some of these budget motels.) Discounts are often available at the more upscale Valley River Inn, which is a very pleasant place to stay. Campsites and rustic digs are east of town on the McKenzie River Highway. As with many Oregon towns, an 8 percent room tax is added to the tariff.

Under $50

The **Eugene Whiteaker Hostel** (970 W. 3rd Ave., 541/343-3335, www.eugenewhiteakerhostel.com, $22 and up) has men's and women's dorms and private rooms in a house that was converted to a hostel in 2006. This is definitely a hippie-style place in a funky, convenient neighborhood.

Of the budget hotels near downtown, the **Timbers Motel** (1015 Pearl St., 541/343-3345 or 800/643-4167, www.timbersmotel.net, $49 and up) is a good bet with clean and relatively attractive rooms. Note that it's just down the block from the Greyhound station, which unfortunately means there can be some pretty scruffy-looking folks on the sidewalks. But it's also practically across the street from breakfast at the Palace Bakery.

$50-100

Downtown Motel (361 W. 7th Ave., www.downtownmotel.com, $60 and up) is a conveniently located bargain. Don't expect luxury, and enjoy the 1950s ambiance of this classic court motel. Nearby, the **Courtesy Inn** (345 W. 6th Ave., 888/259-8481, www.courtesyinn-neugene.com, $60 and up) is another good bet; it's a couple of blocks from the Hult Center and within easy walking distance of restaurants.

The **Best Western New Oregon Motel** (1655 Franklin Blvd., 541/683-3669, $90 and up) is a good choice for visiting parents of U. of O. students or for folks in town to attend a sporting or cultural event. It's located right across the street from the Registration Office and dormitories. This place offers a fair number of amenities (spa, pool, fitness room, racquetball court) and well-appointed rooms. Behind the hotel lie Alton Baker Park and a walking and jogging trail along the river.

$100-150

There are a couple of good B&Bs and a small inn in the downtown and campus neighborhoods of Eugene. The █ **Campbell House** (252 Pearl St., 541/343-1119, www.campbellhouse.com, $129 and up, breakfast included) is a 19-room Victorian in the historic east Skinner Butte neighborhood. Proximity to the Fifth Street Market and the river, as well as the sophistication of a European-style pension, makes this antique-filled 1892 gem a good lodging choice.

Downtown, **C'est la Vie Inn** (1006 Taylor St., 541/302-3014 or 866/302-3014, $140 and up) is a charming and meticulously renovated Queen Anne Victorian with four comfortable guest rooms.

The upstairs of a popular eatery just a block from campus, the **Excelsior Inn** (754 E. 13th Ave., 541/485-1206, www.excelsiorinn.com, $99 and up, breakfast included) offers 14 elegant bed-and-breakfast guest rooms featuring antiques, cherry furniture, marble tile, and fresh-cut flowers. An elevator makes the rooms wheelchair accessible.

$150-200

The best standard motel in town is █ **Valley River Inn** (1000 Valley River Way, Valley River Center, 541/687-0123, www.valleyriverinn.com, $150 and up, Web specials often available). Don't be deterred by its location away from downtown in back of a giant shopping mall; the Willamette River is in back of the inn, which provides easy access to the riverside trail network. In fact, it's easier to get downtown along the bike path than it is to drive. It's also a good place to stay if you're traveling with a dog; the inn is pet friendly, and the riverside path makes for delightful dog walks. A decent restaurant, a crackling fire in the lobby, and pool and spa facilities add to the allure. If it's in your budget, pony up for a riverside room—the view is worth it.

In the downtown area, the **Eugene Hilton** (66 E. 6th Ave., 541/342-2000 or 800/445-8667, www.hilton.com, $150 and up) is the top high-end hotel and is host to many conferences. It has a great location right across the street from the Hult Center and within easy walking distance of the city's best restaurants. One caveat: If you plan to stay here during Eugene Celebration, bring earplugs if you want to get to sleep before the street party winds down for the night.

Camping

If you're looking for campsites in the covered-bridge country above Cottage Grove, try **Baker Bay** (35635 Shoreview Dr., Dorena, 541/682-2000, $16). Located about 18 miles from Eugene, Baker Bay offers sailboats and motorboats for rent. Take I-5 South to Mosby Creek Road (take the Cottage Grove Exit), turn left, then left again on Row River Road, and then take the right fork.

If you just need a parking lot–style RV campground with a few tent sites, **Eugene Kamping World RV Park** (90932 S. Stuart Way, Coburg, 541/343-4832) is just north of Eugene near the quaint town of Coburg. Take the Coburg Exit off I-5, head west, and you'll find the RV park 1 mile or so down the road.

Between the coast and the Oregon Country Fair grounds, **Triangle Lake Park** (541/927-6189) has 18 sites for $10 per night. Proceed 25 miles northwest from the fairgrounds on Route 126. Take a right onto Territorial Highway,

then a left on Route 36 to Triangle Lake. You'll find the campsites just after the lake.

Fern Ridge Shores (29652 Jeans Rd., Veneta, 541/935-2335, $25) is a quiet family campground 12 miles west of Eugene convenient to the Oregon Country Fair.

RVers, Oregon Country Fair–goers, rock concert attendees, and Scandinavian Fair visitors stay at **Richardson County Park** (25950 Richardson Park Rd., Junction City, 541/935-2005, mid-Apr.–mid-Oct., $20) on the shores of Fern Ridge Reservoir 6 miles northwest of Eugene. The 88 sites with hookups and water can be accessed by taking Clear Lake Road off Route 99 to its intersection with Territorial Road.

FOOD

Eating out in Eugene has long been a delight, thanks to such restaurants as longtime favorite Ambrosia and the highly regarded Marché. You may also be impressed by the staggering array of locally made gourmet products and natural foods available at the markets. As you might have guessed, many of these delectables are foremost organically grown and nutritionally sound. And although it's perhaps not as nutritionally sound as, say, Toby's Tofu Pâté (the spicy version is quite good), be sure to treat yourself to some **Prince Puckler's** ice cream (1605 E. 19th Ave., 541/344-4418).

Fifth Street Market Area

Since it opened in 1997, **(Marché** (296 E. 5th Ave., 541/342-3612, 11:30 A.M.–2 P.M. and 5:30–9 P.M. Sun.–Thurs., 11:30 A.M.–2 P.M. and 5:30–10 P.M. Fri.–Sat., dinner entrées $21–34) has set the standard for fine dining in Eugene. The restaurant, in the ground-floor southwest corner of the Fifth Street Market, is as close to a French bistro as you're going to find in this town, and the food is decidedly French-inflected, with an emphasis on fresh local produce and meat. Don't feel like you have to dress up or take out a second mortgage to eat here. The atmosphere is crisp but not fussy, and if you sit in the bar, you can while away an enjoyable but not particularly expensive evening with drinks and small plates, which can be fairly substantial, such as steak frites with a little salad for $14.50. Another good deal is the $25 three-course set-menu dinner.

For a more casual take on Marché's food, head upstairs in the Fifth Street Market to the **Marché Café** (296 E. 5th Ave., 541/342-3612, 8:30 A.M.–7 P.M. Mon.–Sat., 9 A.M.–6 P.M. Sun., $7–9 for a light meal), where the food spans the hours from late breakfast to early dinner with quiche, tasty open-faced sandwiches, soups, and salads. Marché also operates a café at the Jordan Schnitzer Museum of Art on the university campus.

A couple of blocks from the Fifth Street Market is **Red Agave** (454 Willamette St., 541/683-2206, 5–9 P.M. Mon.–Thurs., 5–10 P.M. Fri.–Sat., small plates $6–12, entrées $14–26), a casual and appealing Nuevo Latino restaurant. Although it can be bustling and loud, the bright colors, pomegranate daiquiris, and friendly staff can quickly put you in a mellow Latin groove. The menu has lots of fish, and it's all more sophisticated and alluring than your standard Baja fish taco. The bar is open late with a bar menu, but not full dinners, available until close.

You'll find vegan food and lefty politics at **Morning Glory Café** (450 Willamette St., 541/687-0709, 7:30 A.M.–3:30 P.M. daily, $5–10). Some menu items do contain dairy, but this is the place to come for a very tasty tempeh sandwich.

In a complex across the street from the Fifth Street Market, **Café Lucky Noodle** (205 E. 5th Ave., 541/484-4777, 11 A.M.–midnight Mon.–Fri., 9 A.M.–midnight Sat.–Sun., $13–20) serves both Asian and Italian noodle dishes as well as breakfast, espresso, and gelato in a airy stylish space. Somehow this works…and although the prices are a bit on the steep side (pad Thai is $13), the food is flavorful and the portions are generous. Lucky Noodle's sister restaurant, **Ring of Fire** (1099 Chambers St., 541/344-6475, 11 A.M.–11 P.M. Mon.–Sat., noon–11 P.M. Sun., $11–16) is also recommended.

Central Downtown Area

After a period of turbulence, including a several-month closure, **Cafe Zenon** (898 Pearl St., 541/684-4000, 11 A.M.–10 P.M. Mon.–Thurs., 11 A.M.–11 P.M. Fri.–Sat., 5–10 P.M. Sun., $16–23) is once again serving lunch and dinner at the corner of Pearl and Broadway. For those who remember the Zenon of old, the menu has been scaled down but is similar, with a multiethnic focus, but the dining room is a bit quieter, thanks to some much-needed soundproofing. This is a convivial and generally affordable place to dine on Thai yam curry ($16) while your companions eat posole and black-bean enchiladas ($17) or roasted rack of lamb ($23).

Near the corner of Pearl and Broadway are several other noteworthy restaurants, including **Full City Coffee** (842 Pearl St., 541/344-0475), several doors down, which can be counted on to sustain you with the best coffee in a town. Famous for its daily grind, this is one of several locations in town. If a light breakfast will do, have a scone at the adjacent **Palace Bakery** (844 Pearl St., 541/484-2435).

At **Ambrosia** (174 Broadway, 541/342-4141, 11:30 A.M.–10 P.M. Mon.–Thurs., 11:30 A.M.–11 P.M. Fri., 4:30–11 P.M. Sat., 4:30–9:30 P.M. Sun., $11–20), antique furnishings and stained glass set the stage for Italian cuisine prepared to suit contemporary tastes. The individual-size wood oven–baked gourmet pizzas, a wonderful calamari appetizer, a great wine list, and northern Italian specialties will make spaghetti and meatballs seem like old hat.

In the heart of downtown, **Poppi's Anatolia** (992 Willamette St., 541/343-9661, 11:30 A.M.–9:30 P.M. Mon.–Thurs., 11:30 A.M.–10 P.M. Fri., 11:30 A.M.–3 P.M. and 5–10 P.M. Sat., 5–9:30 P.M. Sun., $10–16) features Greek and Indian food par excellence. Spicy curries and vindaloo chicken are complemented by saganaki (fried cheese), spanakopita (spinach cheese pie), and gyro sandwiches. The best baklava in town with a shot of ouzo or retsina can finish off a richly flavored and moderately priced repast.

At the southwestern edge of downtown,

C Cafe Soriah (384 W. 13th Ave., 541/342-4410, 11 A.M.–2 P.M. and 5–10 P.M. Mon.–Thurs., 11 A.M.–2 P.M. and 5–11 P.M. Fri., 5–11 P.M. Sat., 5–10 P.M. Sun., $14–32) is a popular choice for a romantic dinner or weekday business lunch. Both its patio for summer outdoor dining and its bar topped a local restaurant poll for ambience, but the Mediterranean–Middle Eastern cuisine is the real attraction. Moussaka and various dishes featuring chicken and lamb with vegetables sautéed in olive oil stand out.

Newman's (1545 Willamette St., 541/344-2371, 11 A.M.–7 P.M. Mon.–Fri., 11 A.M.–6:30 P.M. Sat., $6–8) is a fish market with a walk-up fish-and-chips window. Here you can get gourmet renditions of salmon, halibut, and cod with chips.

A block south from the Vets Club on the corner of Willamette is **Euphoria Chocolate Co.** (6 W. 17th Ave., 541/343-9223), a chocolatier of national repute. Their Grand Marnier truffle and other confections are sold around town. Come here after holidays and buy the bite-size Santas, hearts, and bunnies at reduced prices.

If you just want to grab a bagel and some tofu pâté, stop by the **Kiva** (125 W. 11th Ave., 541/342-8666), a funky but well-stocked natural foods store.

Near Campus

The eateries on the campus periphery are a cut above those found in most college towns. Start the day at **Campus Glenwood** (1340 Alder St., 541/687-0355, 7 A.M.–10 P.M. daily) or at the south-side **Glenwood** (2588 Willamette St., 541/687-8201, 6:30 A.M.–9 P.M. Mon.–Fri., 7 A.M.–9 P.M. Sat.–Sun., $5–10). Although both restaurants are open for three meals a day, breakfast is what keeps people coming back…come prepared for a bit of a wait on weekend mornings.

Tasty inexpensive breakfasts and lunches can be had at **Cafe Siena** (853 E. 13th Ave., 541/344-0300, 8 A.M.–7 P.M. Mon.–Fri., 9 A.M.–4 P.M. Sat.–Sun., $4–8). Breakfast burritos are good, and in the winter,

homemade soup seems to be a lunchtime staple for the regulars.

In the shadow of the campus, the **Excelsior Inn Ristorante** (754 E. 13th Ave., 541/485-1206, lunch and dinner daily, Sunday brunch, $18–28) is an elegant restaurant located in a charming old colonial home. The Italian menu changes with the seasons and might include smoked salmon ravioli with a lemony dill sauce or pan-seared sea scallops dusted with porcini powder, topped with tomato relish, served with polenta. Although the Excelsior is very close to campus, it draws a much older crowd; when you see students here, they're often with their parents, who may be staying in the inn upstairs.

South of Downtown

Sundance Natural Foods (748 E. 24th Ave., 541/345-6153) features excellent selections of wine and organic produce. Sundance's fresh salad bar and hot buffet are a good deal. Just around the corner from Sundance, find **Humble Bagels** (2435 Hilyard St., 541/484-4497), a landmark Eugene eatery.

Dinner on the outside deck at **C Beppe & Gianni's Trattoria** (1646 E. 19th Ave., 541/683-6661, 5–9 P.M. Sun.–Thurs., 5–10 P.M. Sat.–Sun., $14–21) is one of Eugene's coveted summertime dining experiences. The menu features homemade pastas with light northern Italian cream- or olive oil–based sauces graced by fresh vegetables, meats, or fish. Try the cappelli di vescovo (bishop hats)—pasta stuffed with Swiss chard, prosciutto, and cheese in a brown-butter sage sauce.

Whitaker Neighborhood

A quarter mile west of center city is Blair Boulevard and the Whitaker neighborhood. In recent years, a budget restaurant row has been developing in what had been in previous decades a strip of fast-food places and greasy spoons. These places, for the most part, are easy on the pocketbook while offering an interesting variety of cuisines.

One of the neighborhood highlights is the **Pizza Research Institute** (530 Blair Blvd.,

541/343-1307, 5–9:30 P.M. daily, $12–18), which has the most innovative pizza in town. In this case, innovation equals excellence—try the chef's choice, which is invariably tasty. PRI, which serves only veggie pies, has a friendly, spunky feel that's thoroughly Eugenian. The pie with Granny Smith apples, smoked Gouda, and roasted walnuts may be life-changing.

Vegetarians can get a good inexpensive meal at **Laughing Planet Café** (760 Blair Blvd., 541/868-0668, 11 A.M.–10 P.M. daily, $5–8). A bean burrito will fill you up, but daring diners will order the dish called soylent green.

A couple of blocks south across 7th Street is a concentration of eateries including **La Tiendita/Taco Loco** (900 Blair Blvd., 541/683-9171, 11 A.M.–9 P.M. Mon.–Sat., 4–8 P.M. Sun., $4–10), serving up locally renowned tamales and other south-of-the-border specialties adjacent to a store devoted to Latino foodstuffs. Low prices, huge portions, and down-home Mexican and El Salvadoran specialties (try the *pupusas*) draw a large takeout clientele at lunch.

On the east side of Blair Boulevard on 7th Street is **Full Boat Cafe** (830 W. 7th Ave., 541/484-2722, 11 A.M.–8 P.M. daily, $6–10), a fish market with an attached café. The array of fish-and-chips is noteworthy for its freshness and the tasty and nontraditional tartar sauces. The attached fish market sells the freshest Dungeness crab in town, excellent smoked salmon, and microbrews.

North of the Willamette

Although **Sweetwaters** (1000 Valley River Way, 541/687-0123, $19–36) is basically a fancy hotel restaurant, it is an easy and pretty tasty bet for those staying at the Valley River Inn, and its riverside outdoor deck might offer Eugene's most delightful dining experience on a warm summer night. Be sure to take a sweater—it cools down fast at night.

Vying with Sweetwaters for Eugene's most scenic restaurant river frontage is the McMenamins' **North Bank** (22 Club Rd., 541/343-5622, 11 A.M.–11 P.M. Mon.–Thurs., 11 A.M.–midnight Fri.–Sat., noon–11 P.M. Sun.,

$8–20). With an outdoor deck, picturesque windows overlooking the Willamette, and a moderately priced menu of quality pub grub featuring everything from eggplant sandwiches to the Communication Breakdown Burger, this is a place to experience how Oregon's preeminent brewpub-meisters have made dining fun. Should wintertime mist obscure the river views, you'll appreciate the penchant of the Brothers M for eccentric woodwork and wistful murals.

INFORMATION

Find info about Eugene at **Travel Lane County** (754 Olive St., 800/547-5445, www.visitlanecounty.org). Also useful is the Planet Eugene website (www.planeteugene.com).

The **Smith Family Bookstore** (768 E. 13th Ave., 541/345-1651, and 525 Willamette St., 541/343-4717) purveys an excellent collection of used books. The **University of Oregon Bookstore** (13th Ave. and Kincaid St., 541/346-4331) has a good selection of new titles and periodicals.

The main local public-radio station, KLCC (89.7 FM), has programming ranging from new-wave jazz to blues. It also has a dynamic news department. The University of Oregon station KWAX (90.1 FM) provides continuous classical music.

Eugene Weekly (1251 Lincoln St., 541/484-0519, www.eugeneweekly.com) has the best entertainment listings in Eugene. At the beginning of each season, the magazine's *Chow* edition will point you in the direction of Eugene's hot restaurants. This publication is available free at commercial establishments all over town.

GETTING THERE AND AROUND

If you're in your own car or on a bike, remember (1) the campus is in the southeastern part of town; (2) 1st Avenue parallels the Willamette River; and (3) Willamette Street divides the city east and west. Navigation is complicated by many one-way roads and dead-ends. Look for alleyways that allow through traffic to avoid getting stuck.

Amtrak (4th and Willamette, 541/344-6265, www.amtrak.com) offers once-daily service both north to Portland and Seattle and south to Sacramento, Oakland, and Los Angeles on the *Coast Starlight*. There are also high-speed trains heading north to Portland daily. In addition, Amtrak runs several express buses each day between Portland and Eugene.

Greyhound (9th Ave. and Pearl St., 800/231-2222) is the other major mode of long-distance public transport, heading south to San Francisco or north to Portland several times daily from Eugene. Typical fares from Eugene to Portland are $17 one-way.

Around town, **Lane Transit District** (541/687-5555, www.ltd.org, $1.50) has canopied pavilions displaying the bus timetables downtown. All buses are equipped with bike racks.

The **Eugene Airport** (541/682-5430, www.eugene-or.gov) is a 20-minute drive northwest from downtown. Just get on the Delta Highway off Washington Street and follow the signs. United Express, Horizon, and America West Express all operate flights in and out of Eugene. There is no city bus service to the airport. **OmniShuttle** (541/461-7959, www.omnishuttle.com, $21.50 from downtown) provides door-to-door shuttle service to and from Eugene Airport to various points in Lane County. **Budget Taxi** (541/683-8294) can also take you where you need to go (airport runs start at $15). **Rental car companies** Avis, Budget, Hertz, and Enterprise also have kiosks at the airport.

The McKenzie River Highway

From I-5 near Eugene, reach this scenic road by taking I-105 east. Take a left at the end of the interstate near the outskirts of Springfield and you will be on the McKenzie River Highway. There are four lanes for a couple of miles, and this is one of your best chances to ease by any slow-moving vehicles. However, beware of the highway patrol on the road—it's easy to end up with a ticket!

Just past where the four lanes merge into two, the McKenzie River Recreation Area begins. For the next 60 miles you will not see any major population centers, as most of the towns consist of little more than a post office. However, you will see beautiful views of the blue-green McKenzie River with heavily forested mountains, frothy waterfalls, jet-black lava beds, and snowcapped peaks as a backdrop. The river was named for Donald Mackenzie, a member of the Astor Pacific Company, who explored the region in 1812.

The first 15 miles of the McKenzie River Highway pass through many fruit and nut orchards (primarily apples, cherries, and filberts), Christmas-tree farms, and berry patches.

McKenzie River farmers enjoy plentiful water supplies from the McKenzie diversion canal, as well as fertile soils and a mild climate.

The Leaburg Dam signals your entry into the middle section of the McKenzie, where there are many vacation homes. A total of six dams on the McKenzie provide power, irrigation, and what the Army Corps of Engineers calls "fish enhancement." A favorite haunt of fishing enthusiasts, the mellow waters of the middle McKenzie teem with trout, steelhead, and salmon. You'll notice many driftboats parked in driveways. These boats have bows at both ends to prevent water inundation from either front or back. Mild white-water rafting and driftboat fishing are popular here, and there are many local guides and outfitters ready to help you float your expeditions.

The Willamette National Forest boundary is near Blue River. Huge old-growth Douglas firs usher the clear blue waters of the McKenzie through the mountains. The McKenzie River National Recreation Trail and many of its counterparts also feature waterfalls, mountain lakes, or lava formations a short trek from the road. In addition to the myriad recreational opportunities, hot springs, quality accommodations, and a dearth of crowds give you the western slopes of the Cascades at their finest.

SIGHTS
Aufderheide National Scenic Byway

One of the nation's first 50 National Scenic Byways, the 58-mile Aufderheide Drive links Route 126 to Route 58 near Oakridge. You'll find the Aufderheide turnoff (Forest Service Rd. 19) at mile marker 45.9 about 5 miles east of Blue River. The road winds along the south fork of the McKenzie River, crests the pass, and then follows the north fork of the middle fork of the Willamette River down to Oakridge and Route 58. Sights along the way include the Delta Old-Growth Grove Nature Trail, Terwilliger (a.k.a. Cougar) Hot Springs, the spectacular Willamette River Gorge, and the Westfir covered bridge.

© BILL MCRAE

The upper McKenzie River is a magical place.

Terwilliger (Cougar) Hot Springs

If you'd like to try a hot springs in a natural setting, head for Terwilliger Hot Springs, located in a forested canyon at the end of a 0.25-mile trail. Hot water bubbles up out of the earth at 116°F and flows down through a series of log and stone pools, each one a few degrees cooler than the previous one. A series of access steps and railings have also been built to help you get to the various soaking ponds. The local custom is to forgo the option of clothing.

To get there, take the Aufderheide Drive from Route 126 south toward Cougar Reservoir. The trailhead for the hot springs on the west (right) side of the road is marked by a sign just past mile marker 7. You can park in a large lot on the east side of the road about 500 feet past the trailhead (alongside the reservoir). Parking alongside the road is prohibited (and enforced) from sunset to sunrise 1 mile from the trailhead. A $5-per-person day-use fee is required, and it has enabled this place to be well maintained.

The several pools in this tranquil forest setting can be overcrowded on weekends. Although this hot spring offers an exceptionally nice soaking experience, it can occasionally attract an unsavory crowd. As with all of the more remote and wild hot springs, take a friend.

Proxy Falls

To get to Proxy Falls, follow the old McKenzie Pass road (Rte. 242) from the new McKenzie Pass highway (Rte. 126) for 10 miles. Look for a small hiker-symbol sign on the south side of the road. This is the only marker for the trail to a spectacular pair of waterfalls, Upper and Lower Proxy Falls.

It's an easy 0.5-mile walk to Upper Proxy, an A-plus trail. The trail goes through a lava field and lush forest that changes with the seasons. There are giant rhododendrons that bloom in late spring, tart huckleberries in late summer, and brilliant red foliage from the vine maples in the fall. Take a left at the first fork in the trail. This will take you to Upper Proxy Falls.

A particularly good view of the waterfalls can be found near the giant Douglas fir at the base of the pool.

Now that you've seen Upper Proxy Falls from the bottom up, check out Lower Proxy Falls from the top down. Go back to the fork in the trail and take a left. In less than 0.5 miles you will suddenly be on a ridge looking across a valley at Lower Proxy Falls. A good time to photograph both of these waterfalls is around midday, when the sun's angle best illuminates the water.

Dee Wright Observatory

The Dee Wright Observatory (57600 McKenzie River Hwy., 541/822-3381, on Rte. 242), closed in winter at the first sign on snow, is at McKenzie Pass about halfway between Route 126 and Sisters. Built in the early 1930s as a Civilian Conservation Corps project, it was named for the building's supervisor, who died prior to its completion. The tower windows line up with views of Mount Jefferson, Mount Washington, and two of the Three Sisters, as well as the 8-mile-long, half-mile-wide lava flow that bubbled out of nearby Yapoah a little less than 3,000 years ago. On a clear day, you can even see the tip of Mount Hood.

The 0.5-mile Lava River Trail next to the observatory offers a fine foray into the surrounding hills of rolling black rock. In addition to helpfully placed and concise interpretive placards explaining the lava formations, the trail is wheelchair accessible. But while the walk is easy enough, the 5,300-foot elevation can sometimes make it seem a little more difficult. Note that on Route 242, vehicle length is restricted to a maximum of 35 feet.

Koosah Falls

This cascade is about 20 miles from McKenzie Bridge on Route 126. The visitor facilities here provide wheelchair access and excellent views of this impressive 70-foot-high waterfall on the McKenzie. The blue water bounces and bubbles over and through a basalt formation that

flowed into the McKenzie thousands of years ago. If you look carefully, you can see many small springs flowing from crevices at the base of the waterfall. The blue water may have inspired the name Koosah, which comes from the Chinook word for "sky."

Sahalie Falls

Another beautiful waterfall is only 0.5 mile farther east on Route 126 from Koosah Falls. From McKenzie Bridge, travel east on Route 126 to Road 2672. Follow Road 2672 to Forest Service Road 655. Follow Forest Service Road 655 to the Sahalie Falls Day Use Area. On the trail from Koosah Falls, giant cedar and fir trees line the path. It is only a few yards from the parking lot to the viewpoints of the waterfall. Also the result of a lava dam from the Cascade Range's not-so-distant volcanic past, the river tumbles 100 feet into a green canyon. This is the highest waterfall on the McKenzie River—*sahalie* means "high" in the Chinook dialect. It's said that this waterfall churns out the highest volume of water of any waterfall in the state.

Clear Lake

Just north of Sahalie and Koosah Falls and east of Route 126 is Clear Lake, which forms the headwaters of the McKenzie River. The best way to appreciate this lake, which is indeed remarkably clear, is in a canoe, so that you can paddle out to the northern end of the lake and look down to see the 3,000-year-old underwater forest that was submerged when lava flows dammed the flow of water and created Clear Lake. A campground and a resort are at the lake; the resort rents out canoes.

Sawyer's Cave

This ice cave is on the right just past the junction of Route 126 and U.S. 20, near mile marker 72. You'll need a flashlight and a sweater to explore Sawyer's Cave; watch your head and watch your step. Classified as a lava tube, it's the result of a lava flow that cooled faster on the top and sides, forming a crust.

Underneath, the hotter lava continued to drain downhill, leaving the lava tube behind. There are also small stalactites hanging down from the ceilings, formed from lava drippings. The basalt rock is a poor heat conductor, and like a natural refrigerator it keeps the coolness of winter and night inside the cave. Ice can be found on the floor of the cave during the hottest summer months.

HIKING
Delta Old-Growth Grove Nature Trail

Find this 0.5-mile loop trail through an old-growth ecosystem on the west side of the Aufderheide Byway not far from Route 126. In addition to 650-year-old conifers, you'll see other layers of life from shrubs and ground-cover plants to fish, mammals, birds, and amphibians. Many plant species are clearly marked along the trail.

◖ McKenzie River National Recreation Trail

The McKenzie River National Recreation Trail (Trail 3507) runs for 26.5 miles. It starts just east of the small town of McKenzie Bridge and goes to the Old Santiam Wagon Road, about 3 miles south of the junction of Route 126 and U.S. 20. But don't let the long distance scare you. There are enough access points to let you design treks of three, five, eight, or more miles along this beautiful trail. It is hard to say which section of the footpath is the best, as each portion has its own charms; the following highlights give you a sample of what to expect.

Start at the top of the McKenzie River Trail at the Old Santiam Wagon Road. Completed in the early 1860s, this was the first link of the route from the mid–Willamette Valley to central and eastern Oregon. Way stations were established a day's journey apart to assist the pioneers along their weary way. Although most of these primitive establishments are no more, some of the historic buildings have survived and are still used today by backpackers. There isn't much left of the Old Santiam Wagon

Road either, as much of it was destroyed with the construction of Route 126. However, a seven-mile stretch remains from Route 126 through the rugged lava country to the Pacific Crest Trail. A short walk on this former road to the promised land helps you to appreciate both the hardiness of the pioneers and the comforts of modern travel.

From the Old Santiam Wagon Road, the McKenzie River Trail surveys many remarkable volcanic formations. Lava flows over the last few thousand years have built dams, created waterfalls, and even buried the river altogether. Koosah and Sahalie Falls were also created by lava dams, and the view of these white-water cascades from the McKenzie River Trail is much different than the version accessible from the highway. Another interesting sight is the Tamolitch Valley, where the McKenzie gradually sinks beneath the porous lava, disappearing altogether until it reemerges three miles later at cobalt-colored Tamolitch Pool.

Lava blankets the ground near the McKenzie River National Recreation Trail.

This area is accessible only on the National Recreation Trail.

If possible, arrange your McKenzie outing with friends and run a two-car shuttle; McKenzie River Mountain Resort (541/822-6272) runs a shuttle service. Also keep in mind that hikes starting at the upper end of the trail take advantage of the descending elevation. Mountain bikes are allowed on all sections of the McKenzie River Trail.

Robinson Lake Trail

The 0.25-mile Robinson Lake Trail takes you to a heart-shaped lake with some fishing and swimming. To get there, take Route 126 about 16 miles east of McKenzie Bridge and turn right onto Robinson Lake Road. Be on the lookout for logging trucks and rocks on the gravel road. Follow the signs marked Forest Service Road 2664. At the unmarked junction, drive straight onto the red pumice road (Forest Service Rd. 2664) and continue until you reach the parking area. It takes about 10 minutes to drive the 4 miles in. The easy hiking trail is in good condition; the left fork takes you to the center shore of Robinson Lake. The shallow lake warms up considerably during the summer, making a swim all the more inviting.

RAFTING

The McKenzie River becomes navigable at the Olallie campground, about 11 miles east of McKenzie Bridge. Between the Olallie campground and the town of Blue River, there are seven public boat launches, including at Paradise and McKenzie Bridge campgrounds. Expect to encounter Class II and III rapids along the Upper McKenzie. Many local outfitters can guide you down the river.

McKenzie River Adventures (541/822-3806 or 800/832-5858, www.mckenzieriveradventures.com) has half-, full-, and two-day white-water rafting trips May–September. The half-day (four-hour) trip is $80 adults, $60 children, lunch included; the full-day (seven-hour) trip is $100 adults, $80 children, lunch included. The cruises range 7–18 miles and take

in some Class II and III rapids. Reservations are recommended.

Destination Wilderness (541/549-1336 or 800/423-8868, www.wildernesstrips.com) floats the McKenzie March–October. Half-day trips are $75 adults, $65 children; full-day $95 adults, $75 children; and two-day $295 adults, and $265 children.

Oregon Whitewater Adventures (39620 Deerhorn Rd., Springfield, 541/746-5422 or 800/820-7238, www.oregonwhitewater.com) offers guided half-day trips for $60, full-day trips for $90, and a two-day overnighter for $290. All necessary gear and transportation back to your car are included.

FISHING

Sure it's crowded, but scenic beauty and the chance to bag a five-trout limit lines 'em up on one of the state's best trout streams. Unless you can get a driftboat, access is limited. On weekends, driftboats and rafters vie for space. You can cast worms or spinners, though you're better off using flies when you're fishing off a boat for rainbow trout April–October. Anglers might want to book a trip with **Helfrich Outfitters** (541/741-1905 or 800/507-9889, www.helfrichoutfitter.com, full-day trip $350–375). Consult the **Oregon Guides and Packers Directory** for other local guides (531 SW 13th St., Bend 97702, 541/617-2876 or 800/747-9552, www.ogpa.org). The best pools tend to be west of Blue River, but it's harder to get to them because of private landholdings. Be sure to check for rules and regulations before you go fishing; the Department of Fish and Wildlife (503/947-6000, www.dfw.state.or.us) can give you the information you need.

OTHER ACTIVITIES

Golf

If you like to play golf, you should plan your vacation around a visit to **Tokatee Golf Club** (54947 Rte. 126, Blue River, 541/822-3220 or 800/452-6376, www.tokatee.com, Feb.–mid-Nov., $24 for nine holes, $42 for 18 holes, online specials often available). Consistently rated among the top 25 courses in the United States by *Golf Digest,* Tokatee is a marriage of golf and wilderness beauty that creates a unique and satisfying experience. Good for all levels of experience; every hole has its own challenge. No houses are on the fairways to obstruct the knockout views of the forested mountains and the Three Sisters Wilderness.

Mountain Biking

In the upper sections of the McKenzie, most of the usable trails gain elevation rapidly due to the steep terrain and make for very challenging biking. The most popular route is the **McKenzie River Trail.** Contact the McKenzie River Ranger District (503/822-3381) for detailed information. McKenzie River Mountain Resort (541/822-6272) has bikes for rent and runs a shuttle service for trail users.

ACCOMMODATIONS

You know when you cross over the McKenzie on the 165-foot-long Goodpasture Covered Bridge (circa 1938), the most photographed bridge in Oregon, that you're headed for someplace interesting. A great place for families, including pets, and those who want to get away from the noise of the McKenzie highway is the **Wayfarer Resort** (46725 Goodpasture Rd., Vida, 541/896-3613 www.wayfarerresort.com, $105 and up), featuring over a dozen cabins on the McKenzie and glacier-fed Marten Creek. Accommodating 1–6 people, the cabins have porches with barbecues overlooking the water, full kitchens, and lots of wood paneling. Two larger units can sleep eight and are equipped with all the amenities. Children can enjoy fishing privileges in the resort's private trout pond while the folks play on the resort's tennis court. All guests are welcome to supplement their menus with pickings from the Wayfarer's organic gardens and berry patch. In the summer, advance reservations are a must for this popular retreat.

Heaven's Gate Cottages (50055 McKenzie Hwy., Vida, 541/822-3214, www.heavens-gaterivercottages.com, $105 and up) offers housekeeping cabins right on the McKenzie. Although the cabins are sandwiched between the highway and the river, the unspoiled riverside view more than compensates for the traffic (which drops off considerably by nightfall). One cabin is right over a good fishing hole, and night lights illuminate the rapids for your contemplation. A fireplace adds an additional romantic touch. These cabins may be old, small, and semirustic, but their riverside location helps overcome a multitude of issues.

The former Blue River ranger station has been repurposed as the lodge for the **McKenzie River Mountain Resort** (51668 Blue River Dr., Blue River, 541/822-6272, www.rivermountainresort.com, $50 lodge room, $160 and up cabin); vacation cabins used to house the rangers. The bunkhouse-style lodge rooms are fairly Spartan but very clean and OK for someone who is planning to spend the day fishing or hiking; it's common for groups to rent the entire lodge.

Although **Harbick's Country Inn** (54791 Rte. 126, Blue River, 541/822-3805, $70 and up) may not be as charming as some of the other lodgings along the McKenzie, it is located within walking distance of one of the finest public golf courses in the country, Tokatee. Because of this, it's quite popular—reserve in advance.

The C **Cedarwood Lodge** (56535 McKenzie Hwy./Rte. 126, McKenzie Bridge, 541/822-3351, www.cedarwoodlodge.com, Apr.–Oct., $105 and up) is tucked away in a grove of old cedars just outside the town of McKenzie Bridge. The lodge has nine vacation housekeeping cottages that feature fully equipped kitchens, bathrooms (with showers), fireplaces (wood provided), and portable barbecues. This is a sweet place to spend a couple of nights, particularly in those units with decks on the river.

Unfortunately, fire claimed the historic lodge at the **Log Cabin Inn** (Rte. 126, McKenzie Bridge, www.logcabininn.com) in spring of 2006. The beautiful 100-year-old lodge had hosted President Hoover, Clark Gable, the

Duke of Windsor, and a host of Oregon families over the years. The lodge is being rebuilt and is supposed to be open for business by summer 2010. It's worth checking into this! The inn is located at mile marker 51 near the intersection of Route 126 and Route 242.

Across the road from the Log Cabin Inn, spacious and attractive modern cabins at **Inn at the Bridge** (56393 McKenzie Hwy., McKenzie Bridge, 541/743-2012, www.mckenzie-river-cabins.com, $175) are open year-round.

Belknap Lodge and Hot Springs (59296 Belknap Springs Rd., McKenzie Bridge, 541/822-3512, www.belknaphotsprings.com) offers lodge rooms, cabins, camping, and access to two hot springs swimming pools. The lodge rooms range $100–185 per couple; bathtubs are plumbed with hot springs water. The five cabins range $65–400; the least expensive are very rustic but pet-friendly. Campsites are $25–30. The main attraction on the property is Belknap Springs. The water, which contains 26 different minerals, is gently filtered piping hot into a swimming pool on the south bank of the McKenzie. The property is clean, the scenery is beautiful, and the price is right. For $7, drop-in visitors can use the lower pool for an hour; a day pass is $12 and just what the doctor ordered to ease the aching muscles from that killer hike or the ski marathon. But don't wait too long to fill this prescription—the pool closes at 9 P.M. If you forget your towel, you can rent one.

Camping

The following campgrounds are under the jurisdiction of the Willamette National Forest, McKenzie Ranger District (info 541/822-3381, www.fs.fed.us/r6/willamette; reservations 877/444-6777, www.recreation.gov). Many are along the beautiful McKenzie River National Recreation Trail. Its prime location halfway between Eugene and Bend also helps make the area a popular vacation spot during the summer, so advance reservations should be made at least five days in advance. Sites at most of these campgrounds run $12–18 per night; those without piped-in water tend to be free.

A half-mile west of McKenzie Bridge on Route 126 is the 20-site riverside **McKenzie Bridge Campground.** Piped well water, vault toilets, and a boat launch are provided. East of McKenzie Bridge about 3 miles on Route 126 is **Paradise Campground.** Although there are 64 tent/RV (up to 40 feet) campsites, flush and vault toilets, and piped water, only half of the sites are in premium riverside locations. The summer trout fishing here can be very good, and the fireplace grills and wooden tables make it easy to cook and eat a fresh-caught meal. Welcome to paradise!

Olallie Campground is 11 miles from McKenzie Bridge on Route 126 and has 17 sites. Olallie is situated on the banks of the McKenzie River; boating, fishing, and hiking are some of the nearby attractions. Piped water, vault toilets, and picnic tables are provided. A couple of miles past Olallie on Route 126 is **Trailbridge Campground,** located on the north shore of Trailbridge Reservoir. Piped water, vault and flush toilets, and picnic tables are provided at this 26-site campground. Boat docks are close by, and the reservoir is noted for its good trout fishing. This campground is first-come, first-served and not on the reservation system; it is open June–October.

Another ideal campground for boating enthusiasts is **Lake's End** on nearby Smith Reservoir. One of the few boat-in campgrounds in Oregon, this park can only be reached via a 2-mile sail across the lake. To get there, take Route 126 for 12 miles northeast of McKenzie Bridge, turn left, and follow Forest Service Road 730 two miles to the south end of the reservoir. Boat across to the north shore for camping. Be sure to take along plenty of water, because the campground does not provide any. You will find, however, picnic tables, vault toilets, and plenty of peace and quiet away from the cars and traffic of the other mainstream parks. Lake's End is open May–September and has no fees or reservations.

On the south shore of Clear Lake, 19 miles

northeast of McKenzie Bridge on Route 126, is **Coldwater Cove Campground.** Piped water, vault toilets, and picnic tables are provided at this 35-site park, open mid-May–mid-October. **Clearlake Resort** (541/967-3917, www.co.linn.or.us/parks/) is adjacent to the campground and has a store, a summer-only café, and rustic cabins ($64 and up, bring cooking utensils and bedding), as well as boat docks, launches, and rentals. Small electric fishingboat motors are the only mechanical means of propulsion allowed here by the Forest Service. The road to the resort closes at the end of September; guests can hike in to rustic cabins during the winter.

A handful of small campgrounds dot Route 242, the old McKenzie Pass road, but none have piped water. In the same area, RVers should take note of **Camp Yale** (58980 Rte. 242, McKenzie Bridge, 541/822-3512), which is operated by nearby Belknap Hot Springs. It is open all year, with full hookups (water, sewer, and electricity) for $35; there are no tent sites. Modern restrooms with hot-water showers are on-site. Camp Yale also offers the only public dump station between Springfield and Sisters.

FOOD

When the restaurant at the Log Cabin Inn burned down, the area lost its most noteworthy restaurant. Restaurants aren't exactly a big deal out here—most overnight visitors are camping or renting cabins with cooking facilities. Near McKenzie Bridge the **Rustic Skillet** (54771 Rte. 126, 541/822-3400, all meals daily) can be likened to a fancy truck stop—just good ol'

American food. Lest this sound like damning with faint praise, we should add the menu is diverse for its genre. Kids (young and old alike) will enjoy a complimentary round of miniature golf with their meal.

There are a couple of dining options in the vicinity of Blue River. Stop at **Takodas** (91806 Mill Creek Rd., 541/822-1153, 7 A.M.–2 P.M. daily, $6–11), located next to Harbick's Country Store, for a sandwich or a burger. In the evening, the neighboring **Holiday Farm Resort** (54455 McKenzie River Dr., 541/822-3725, 5–9 P.M. daily, $18–29) is the area's most elegant restaurant; here you can dine on a house-smoked duck salad or go for steak, seafood, or pasta.

INFORMATION

Read the local news online at http://mckenzie.orenews.com. Wilderness permits, camping, hiking, and mountain biking information are available the **McKenzie River Ranger District** (57600 McKenzie Hwy., McKenzie Bridge, 541/822-3381, www.fs.fed.us/r6/willamette).

GETTING THERE

Amazingly, travelers without cars can get to the McKenzie National Recreation Trail from Eugene via **Lane Transit District** (541/687-5555, www.ltd.org, $1.50). Their route 91 bus starts at Thurston station in Springfield (with frequent bus connections to downtown Eugene) and heads up the McKenzie River Highway. The bus is equipped to carry a couple of bikes. The terminus point is the McKenzie River Ranger Station at McKenzie Bridge.

Oakridge and the Upper Willamette River

Halfway between Eugene and the Cascades' summit on Route 58 lies the town of Oakridge. Lumber, secondary wood products (furniture, toys, etc.), recreation, and tourism support this small community (pop. 3,200) tucked away in a foothill valley of the Cascades. Visitors will find some of the finest wilderness areas in Oregon in this area.

There are over 100 lakes and streams nearby waiting for just about any nimrod to pull out his or her quota of rainbow, German brown, cutthroat, and Dolly Varden trout from the cool waters. A short drive southeast of town, near Willamette Pass, are several Central Oregon gems: Waldo Lake, the Diamond Peak Wilderness Area, and Odell Lake. Wintersports enthusiasts can find excellent downhill skiing at Willamette Pass, which features 18 runs, four chairlifts, a rope tow, and a day lodge. There are plenty of beautiful trails available for Nordic skiers too. If you like to fish, hike, camp, sail, ski, mountain bike, or just hang out in the woods, it's all only minutes away from Oakridge.

SIGHTS
Westfir Covered Bridge

A short distance out of Oakridge on the paved Aufderheide National Scenic Byway is the Westfir Covered Bridge. This bright-red span has the distinction of being the longest covered bridge in Oregon (180 feet) as well as the tallest covered bridge west of the Mississippi. Furthermore, it is likely that it is also the heaviest span of any wood construction bridge due to its Howe trusses, extension rods, and cords. You can see what remains of the Hines Company mill on the opposite side of the bridge; in its heyday it employed 750 people and operated around the clock. You can get a good picture of the bridge from the road as you approach the nearby town of Westfir.

Salt Creek Falls

About 20 miles southeast of Oakridge, just west of Willamette Pass on the way to Odell Lake on Route 58, is Oregon's second-highest waterfall, Salt Creek Falls, which forms the headwaters of the Willamette River. You'll find the pullout on the south side of the highway. The short walk to the viewing area of the 286-foot-high cascade provides a great photo opportunity. Trails access both the top and the bottom of the waterfall for those interested in taking a closer look at this raw display of hydropower.

Hot Springs
McCredie Hot Springs is 10 miles southeast of Oakridge on Route 58 near mile marker 45. A short walk down to Salt Creek brings you to a small hot spring adjacent to the river. This location allows you to enjoy the rush of simultaneously hot and cold water. Depending on how you position yourself, you can take a bath at any temperature you choose—be careful, there are some extremely hot spots. Because it's so close to the road that this place is often busy; many bathe nude here.

Another primitive hot springs in the area is **Meditation Pool** (Wall Creek). It's really more like a warm spring, as the water ranges about 90–104°F, depending on weather conditions. It's a short easy hike in, and the soak is worth the effort. To get there, turn north onto Rose Street from Route 58 in Oakridge. Turn right onto 1st Street, proceed east, and 1st Street will eventually become Forest Service Road 24, paralleling Salmon Creek. About 10 miles out of Oakridge, look for Forest Service Road 1934 on the left (north) side of the road. Approximately 0.5 miles down Forest Service Road 1934 you'll see a trailhead sign (the kind with no name, only two figures hiking) on the west (left) side of the road. Follow the path along Wall Creek about 0.3 miles up to the creek-side pool. East of Oakridge on Route 58 on the south side of the highway is the Greenwater rest area, a beautiful place to take in the laid-back charm of the upper Willamette River.

HIKING
Fall Creek National Recreation Trail

The 14-mile-long Fall Creek National Recreation Trail, about 30 miles southeast of Eugene, is ideal for short day hikes or longer expeditions; several national forest entry/exit points crop up along the way. Another plus is the low elevation of the trail, which makes it accessible year-round. Strolling through the wilderness, you will pass many deep pools, white-water rapids, and over a dozen small streams. Giant Douglas firs, bigleaf maples, vine maples, dogwoods, and red alders are some of the predominant vegetation you'll see along the way. In the spring, visitors are treated to shooting stars, trillium, bleeding heart, and other vibrant wildflowers.

To get there, take Route 58 about 15 miles to Lowell, then go north for 2 miles to the covered bridge at Unity Junction. Take a right onto Forest Service Road 18 (Fall Creek Rd.), and stay to the left of the reservoir. Follow the road for 11 miles to Dolly Varden Campground, where the trail starts. There are five campgrounds en route and three other spur trails that merge into the Fall Creek Trail. **Bedrock Campground** is a particularly popular spot for swimming.

Larison Creek Trail

The Larison Creek Trail (Trail 3646) is less than 10 minutes from Oakridge. Multicolored mosses cover the valley floor, and its walls simulate a brush-stroked backdrop to stands of old-growth fir. Further contrast is supplied by waterfalls and swimming holes. The mild grade and low elevation of this trail make it accessible year-round. To get there, take Route 58 to Oakridge. Turn onto Kitson Springs County Road and proceed for 0.5 miles. Turn

right on Forest Service Road 21 and follow it 3 miles to the trailhead, which you'll find on the right side of the road. Note that this trail is shared with mountain bikers.

Tufti Creek Trail

Another good hike close to Oakridge is the Tufti Creek Trail (Trail 3624). This easy 0.5-mile trail winds through large Douglas firs and cedars and overlooks Hills Creek Gorge. There are many small waterfalls and deep swimming holes along the way. This trail is also accessible year-round.

To get there, take Route 58 to Oakridge. Turn onto Kitson Springs County Road and proceed for about 1 mile. Turn left onto Forest Service Road 23 and follow it for 6 miles. This will take you along the northeast bank of Hills Creek Lake and on past Kitson Hot Springs (which is also worthy of investigation). Look for the trailhead sign on the right, about 1 mile past the hot springs.

◖ OAKRIDGE MOUNTAIN BIKING

Mountain biking has become incredibly popular in the Oakridge area, which is not surprising given that there are an estimated 350 miles of single-track within an hour's drive of town. Find information and detailed trail descriptions at www.mtbikeoregon.com.

Novice bikers and families can start with the **Salmon Creek Trail,** which starts in town and heads along generally flat terrain to Salmon Creek Falls.

Also just outside town, starting at Greenwaters Park near the fish hatchery, **Larison Rock** is a thrilling, technical 5-mile downhill ride. Then, unless you've arranged a car shuttle, it's a bit of a slog back to the start. (An easier though longer route back follows Forest Road 2102.)

The nearly 30-mile-long **Middle Fork River Trail** is a good bet for more experienced mountain bikers who want to test their stamina. It starts at the Sand Prairie campground south of town and heads south and east along the Middle Fork of the Willamette River.

Oakridge hosts a couple of mountain-bike events, one in mid-July and the other in August (503/459-4508, www.mtbikeoregon.com, $280) with guided rides of the area's trails, meals, beer, and camping.

Road cyclists needn't avoid Oakridge; the Aufderheide Scenic Byway is an excellent low-traffic paved road along the North Fork of the Willamette River.

ACCOMMODATIONS

There are some reasonable lodging options in the area. The **Bluewolf Motel** (47465 Rte. 58, 541/782-5884, $40 and up) is a small, simple motel with microwaves and refrigerators. The plush place to stay in these parts is the **Best Western Oakridge Inn** (47433 Rte. 58, 541/782-2212 or 800/528-1234, $96), which has 30 spacious guest rooms and a pool, a hot tub, and HBO.

In the former office building of Hines Lumber Company in Westfir, across the street from the covered bridge, is the **Westfir Lodge** (47365 1st St., Westfir, 541/782-3103, www.westfirlodge.com, $80 and up). The building has been tastefully converted into seven guest rooms with English-style bathrooms (each room has its own private bath, but it's across the hall from the bedroom). The house is full of curious Asian antiques, and the pantry used to be the company vault. A full breakfast (try the English bangers) is included.

FOOD

The best coffee, good food (as local and organic as possible), and abundant local charm are at the funky-artsy ◖ **Trailhead Coffeehouse** (47406 Rte. 58, 541/782-2223, 8 A.M.–2 P.M. Tues., 8 A.M.–9 P.M. Wed.–Sun., $8–20), across from the Best Western. Friday and Saturday evenings bring live music, generally an open jam session. It's a great stop for homemade baked goods, sandwiches, wraps, burgers, soups, and salads—call ahead if you want to order a steak.

The other place that's good to know about in town is the **Brewers Union Local 180** (48329 E. 1st St., 541/782-2024, noon–9 P.M. Sun.–Wed., noon–10 P.M. Thurs., noon–9 P.M. Fri.–Sat. summer, noon–9 P.M. Sun., 4–10 P.M. Mon.–Wed., noon–10 P.M. Thurs., noon–11 P.M. Fri.–Sat. winter, $5–11), a British-style public house where it's as easy to settle in with a cup of tea as with a pint of real ale, and you can either read a book or play pool. You can choose between tempeh, spam, and beef for your burger.

INFORMATION

The **chamber of commerce** (44284 Rte. 58, 541/782-4146, www.oakridgechamber.com) offers information on the area.

Additional information on biking, hiking, camping, and the Aufderheide National Scenic Byway can be obtained from the **Middle Fork Ranger Station** (46375 Rte. 58, Westfir, 541/782-2283, www.fs.fed.us/r6/willamette).

MOON EUGENE, SALEM &
THE WILLAMETTE VALLEY

Avalon Travel
a member of the Perseus Books Group
1700 Fourth Street
Berkeley, CA 94710, USA
www.moon.com

Editor: Tiffany Watson
Series Manager: Kathryn Ettinger
Copy Editor: Christopher Church
Graphics and Production Coordinator:
    Lucie Ericksen
Cover Designer: Kathryn Osgood
Map Editor: Albert Angulo
Cartographers: Kat Bennett, Chris Markiewicz,
    Michelle Trame, Brice Ticen

ISBN: 978-1-59880-551-2

Some photos and illustrations are used by permission and are the property of the original copyright owners.

Front cover photo: Vineyards rolling over hills in moody early evening light, Willamette Valley © Donald Gruener/istockphoto.com
Title page photo: Willamette Valley in the springtime © Judy Jewell

Printed in the United States

ABOUT THE AUTHORS

Judy Jewell & W. C. McRae

Between the two of them, Judy Jewell and Bill McRae have lived in and traveled around Oregon for more than 50 years. During this time, they've also strayed out of state to research and write Moon Handbooks to Montana, Utah, and southern Utah's national parks (a.k.a. Zion and Bryce).

Judy graduated from Reed College and worked at Portland's renowned Powell's Books for fourteen years as a book buyer and manager, until she decided to leave to write travel books. When she's not traveling around the West, she now works as a technical and scientific editor and a yoga teacher. Bill has written for Frommer's, Lonely Planet, and Mobile Guides, and has provided content for *1000 Places to See in the USA and Canada Before You Die*. He has also edited books for National Geographic and provided content for websites like GORP.com and Expedia.com.

Judy and Bill both live in Portland, Oregon.